The Art of Rehearsal

Related titles from Bloomsbury Methuen Drama

The Collected Essays of Arthur Miller
Arthur Miller
ISBN 978-1-4725-9174-6

Devising Theatre with Stan's Cafe
Mark Crossley and James Yarker
ISBN 978-1-4742-6704-5

Disobedient Theatre
Chris Johnston
ISBN 978-1-3500-0759-8

Edward Bond: The Playwright Speaks
Edward Bond and David Tuaillon
ISBN 978-1-4725-7006-2

Meyerhold on Theatre
Edward Braun, edited by Jonathan Pitches
ISBN 978-1-4742-3020-9

New Dramaturgy: International Perspectives on Theory and Practice
Edited by Katalin Trencsényi and Bernadette Cochrane
ISBN 978-1-4081-7708-2

Simon Stephens: A Working Diary
Simon Stephens
ISBN 978-1-4742-5141-9

Steppenwolf Theatre Company of Chicago
John Mayer
ISBN 978-1-4742-3945-5

Theatre and Adaptation: Return, Rewrite, Repeat
Edited by Margherita Laera
ISBN 978-1-4081-8472-1

The Art of Rehearsal

Conversations with Contemporary Theatre Makers

Edited by Barbara Simonsen

Bloomsbury Methuen Drama
An imprint of Bloomsbury Publishing Plc
B L O O M S B U R Y
LONDON • OXFORD • NEW YORK • NEW DELHI • SYDNEY

Bloomsbury Methuen Drama
An imprint of Bloomsbury Publishing Plc

50 Bedford Square
London
WC1B 3DP
UK

1385 Broadway
New York
NY 10018
USA

www.bloomsbury.com

BLOOMSBURY and the Diana logo are trademarks of Bloomsbury Publishing Plc

First published 2017

British Library Cataloguing-in-Publication Data
A catalogue record for this book is available from the British Library.

ISBN: HB: 978-1-474-29200-9
PB: 978-1-474-29201-6
ePDF: 978-1-474-29202-3
eBook: 978-1-474-29199-6

Library of Congress Cataloging-in-Publication Data
A catalog record for this book is available from the Library of Congress.

Cover design: Louise Dugdale
Cover image © Jasper Juinen / Getty images

Typeset by Fakenham Prepress Solutions, Fakenham, Norfolk NR21 8NN
Printed and bound in Great Britain

Contents

List of illustrations

Acknowledgements

First of all, a huge thank you to all the artists who so generously shared their thoughts and experiences with us. I am so very grateful to have been on this expedition with Isabelle Reynaud and Deborah Vlaeymans – what a fantastic journey of discovery we have had. And thank you to the Danish Arts Council, Nordic Culture Point, the Aarhus Municipality and the Wilhelm Hansen Foundation for their support to the making of the interviews. I also want to thank everyone at Entré Scenen and Bora-Bora, Aarhus, for all their support around Laboratoriet and the Rehearsal Matters project.

A big, warm thank you to my colleague at Seachange Lab Fabienne Pauly for invaluable help with texts and notes and facts and German transcripts. And for never-failing encouragement. To Paul Allain and Peter Boenisch for helping to make this book happen, and to the editorial team at Bloomsbury Methuen Drama, especially the ever patient and cheerful Mark Dudgeon, for advice and guidance.

And last, but not least, to my darling husband who strangely still and always believes that I can do anything I dream of.

Preface

There are very few books about the process of directing, so such a collection of interviews with a range of European and North American theatre directors is particularly welcome. The mechanisms of directing remain hidden and elusive for many reasons, not least the issue of access to rehearsals but also the difficulty of condensing or fixing such a complex process of development – from the tiny seed of an idea to a 'finished' performance, involving along the way preparation, multiple collaborations, intuitive choices and worked-out plans as well as a myriad of emotions, challenges and practical solutions besides. Perhaps a conversation is the best way to capture some of this. Accordingly, these interviews do an important job of letting readers inside the heads of a range of directors, some very well known and established, some less familiar, in a systematic and organized way, bringing relative order to the disorder of creativity. Chaos is a notion that crops up repeatedly and while it normally carries negative connotations, each of these artists here considers it a familiar friend.

The book is refreshing not just for overturning the many assumptions we might have about what directing is (consider how far these interviews move us away from the idea of a director interpreting and staging plays) but also for its language. It is surprising how rarely those being interviewed use terms that are common currency in academic circles, like devising, physical action, practice as research, actor training, scenography. Instead the vocabulary is more personal, pragmatic, daily and immediate, capturing their doubts, discoveries, hopes, dreams and maxims, and the lively spirit of curiosity that drives them all to make performance in testing circumstances.

The eighteen interviewees discuss a range of modes of performance and geopolitical contexts with the main focus on directing theatre and a strong emphasis on Europe, where fourteen of the directors are based (the other four are in the United States of America). The interviewers are not so much concerned with extracting details of funding or educational backgrounds or enumerating their productions (readers can easily research and discover such facts themselves). These conversations float relatively free of context and time and yet are absolutely focused on the nuts and bolts of performance-making. Beyond the idea of the necessary creative chaos, three Ts appear to be fundamental to them all – time, a team and trust.

The interviewers' questioning is consistent, giving a helpful shape and structure to the book, but it is never rigid. I was reminded of what one of the interviewees, theatre director Eugenio Barba, has called the paradox of 'consistent inconsistency', referring to one of the 'extra-daily' principles of performance. In this way the interviews reveal a diverse range of answers and reflections depending on where the line of enquiry takes them and each director's priorities. And while there is breadth and fluidity, these artists' rigour and dedication radiates throughout.

Reading across the interviews, it soon becomes apparent that similar issues arise everywhere in the world: the constant need to adapt, to react in the moment, to improvise; the sacrifices required (personal and financial amongst many others); and the pleasure that investigating with others in a small room affords. Their formative paths are extremely diverse but they all have in common a daunting scale of (often international) collaboration and the careful negotiation of freedom and constraints. You won't put this book down without feeling huge admiration and respect for all of them: and not just for the director who somewhat ironically hates rehearsals or the one who occasionally performs in his own work and has decided to never take another curtain call.

None of the interviews provide a blueprint for how to direct, but of more value is that they account for what directing involves, what it costs (in non-material terms) and that they give vital insights into this activity which is at the heart of our field and on which it so keenly depends. Here we get behind closed doors, hear the directors' thought processes and can begin to envisage how they work and live. More valuable than facts, we learn about the feeling of directing, its churn and weave, as we momentarily share the directors' emotional and imaginative forays, always underscored by awareness of the need to be extremely pragmatic. This focus on feeling and common values has never felt more important than it does in the emotional turmoil that swirls around as I write this in the immediate aftermath of the 'Brexit' referendum in Britain. My position as co-director of the European Theatre Research Network based at the University of Kent, the UK's 'European University', has never felt so contested and yet so important. This book provides solace in dark times. These artistic stories speak to us all across borders and serve as a reminder of how good art can unite, enrich, teach and challenge in equal measure.

We should then be grateful to Laboratoriet/Seachange Lab for doing such a service for our academic and professional communities in bringing these tales and impressions to our attention. We should celebrate their pan-European and international outlook. Their concern with the conjunction of research and practice means that the book is open, fresh and enquiring yet also decidedly useful. I wondered if these interviews are perhaps partly so compelling because directors are above all expert technicians of storytelling, their lives dedicated to shaping the dramaturgy of narratives and experience. In these stories we can hear, feel and relish this expertise. I invite you to read on and make up your own mind.

Paul Allain
University of Kent, Canterbury, UK
July 2016

Introduction: No one's ever asked me that

Barbara Simonsen

This book springs from a simple research project that started in 2008. It was initiated by Laboratoriet, a small, artist-driven organization based in Aarhus, Denmark, established in 2005 and dedicated to practical artistic research and performing arts experiments.[1] In 2008, we had just finished a series of experiments that had investigated various methods of developing text for theatre and performance. We wanted our next series of experiments to be about the rehearsal process, and we discussed some different possible approaches to such a series – but finally we decided to start by doing a bit of research to get some inspiration and qualify our choices of experiments. We thought we would do a few interviews with different artists, directors, actors, dramaturgs etc. to find out more about what kinds of questions they were working with or maybe struggling with in the rehearsal process, and what their wishes and needs for development and renewal of the process might be.

At the time, Laboratoriet was based at Entré Scenen, a small but lively venue for local independent companies as well as international, touring performances. We had easy access to interesting artists, and so we just started doing interviews about rehearsal process methods and reflections. It only took three or four interviews, however, before we realized that this material that we were collecting had incredible potential. Not just as preliminary research for an experiment series, but as a research project in its own right. It was just stunning how much information and knowledge could be found in interviewing people about what they *do*. Focusing on the process instead of the artistic result, and extracting knowledge from people about their practical methods and concrete experiences of what they do best. Throughout the project we were deeply impressed by how open and honest the interviewees were in answering our questions, both about their best and worst experiences in the rehearsal hall, about their crazy dreams and most beloved ideas, and about their self-criticism and revision of methods and approaches over the years. Many of them would say, 'No one's ever asked me that before' – and they seemed to enjoy the reflections very much. It was simply fascinating stuff. And so we kept on collecting that knowledge.

We were three co-creators of the project that we decided to call Rehearsal Matters: Isabelle Reynaud, Deborah Vlaeymans and myself. Already in 2008, we started travelling to collect interviews with artists from different countries, and every time an international artist or company visited Aarhus, we would be on the spot with our microphone and our two pocket cameras. Since you could say the project started as a bit of a surprise to us, we established the precise framework and the precise questions along the way. When you look at the entire collection you will see that the questions in the earliest interviews vary a bit more than in the later ones. But after a time we decided on five basic questions, the central ones being:

- What is the essential condition for a rehearsal process to succeed?
- What is the biggest problem of the rehearsal process?
- What would you change or try out in the rehearsal process, if anything was possible?

We also asked the artists to describe their methods and typical structures of rehearsal, primarily focusing on what goes on in the rehearsal hall, but of course the understanding of the word rehearsal process is different to different types of artists, whether you are working with manuscripts, devising, theatre or dance, and often there is an overlap between the description of the rehearsal process and the entire creation process. And the fifth question is the one we start the interview by asking the artists: Why they chose to work with theatre, or how they 'ended up' in theatre. Again, it was a surprise to us that a question we took to using as a warm-up to the 'real' interview resulted in answers which were funny, surprising and moving, and which reflect on the artist's work and approach.

Three years and more than thirty interviews later, in 2011, we launched the Rehearsal Matters website with the interviews, some in Danish and some in English, as well as video extracts.[2] The total Rehearsal Matters collection consists, at the moment, of thirty-five interviews with forty artists from eleven countries. Most of them were made between 2008 and 2011, and the three most recent ones are from 2016. The choice of artists in the collection is based on a mixture of personal preferences and chance. As interviewers, the three of us each made a favourite list of artists that we wanted to interview, because they made performances that we admired, or because we knew they had an interesting and unique process, or simply because we thought they would have interesting reflections on processes. Some of these we managed to get in touch with, others we didn't. Sometimes other artists came our way and we jumped at the chance to interview them. We knew that we could never make a complete or representative collection in any sense. So we stuck to personal curiosity and luck as our selection principles. However, an important choice became to focus on interviewing experienced artists with many processes behind them because they gave the most interesting answers to our essential questions. We also would have liked to cover a larger number of countries, but for practical and financial reasons that simply was not possible. On the other hand, the advantage for us in focusing mainly on Scandinavia, Western Europe and North America was that we were able to interview almost all of the artists in their own languages, covering Danish, English, German, French and Dutch between the three of us. We found that it gave a freedom and a richness in the reflections that we might not otherwise have had. With one exception, we have only done interviews face to face, video-recorded, to be able to have a real, in-depth conversation and the live quality captured on tape. Each interview is therefore accompanied by a video extract, and the Rehearsal Matters collection also includes theme videos where we see several of the artists' response to the same question.

This book presents a selection of eighteen Rehearsal Matters interviews, covering a variety of performing arts genres, traditions and approaches, and with some of the most ground-breaking and original artists in their field. They come from eight different countries in Europe and North America, and the youngest of them has a little more than ten years of experience with rehearsal processes, the oldest more than fifty years. They are directors, choreographers or director/performers, but this book is about much more than just directing, since directing is clearly only one of the aspects of a rehearsal process that has to be mastered or handled or thought out. Concrete aspects such as logistics, space, technique, or soft ones such as communication, team psychology and creative structures, or the completely intangible magic of a perfect moment, of letting go, of letting it happen, are all part of the infinitely complex mechanisms of rehearsal. The artists' reflections range from general principles, ideals and values, to the most concrete examples of events and conversations: from the crystal clear to the bewildering and self-contradictory. It is an interesting and important point to remember that the information that we have access to in this book is not the artists' work processes, it is what they *say* about their work processes. It is how they describe them. It does not tell us anything about how their performers or collaborators would describe them, nor how we would describe what we saw happening in the rehearsal hall, if we were there. A study to compare those three different angles would of course give us more information, or rather a different kind of information. What the interviews provide is the communication of a complex interface, so to speak, between what the person wants to do, what he or she is able to do, and what he or she perceives him- or herself as doing, in an artistic, collective process of theatre. The subjective angle is at the same time one of the reasons for the richness, the depth and even the direct usefulness of the knowledge provided, especially if you as reader are actively involved in similar artistic processes. Because of course acquiring a skill is not just about learning to use a certain objectively defined method, but also about knowing how it is useful to think about it and how it feels when it works or doesn't work, or what important goal it may serve to achieve. The subjective view of an artistic process highlights certain aspects and hides others very effectively, but even in that there is information. The video extracts of the interviews are also a helpful companion to understand more about the complex whole of the person and the reflections, and the videos belonging to the interviews in this book can be found on Drama Online.[3]

In the beginning the working title of the project was 'Utopia'. We were expecting the most important answers from the artists to be the answers to the question: What would you change or try out in the rehearsal process, if anything was possible? With the follow-up question: What are your utopian wishes for the rehearsal process? It came as a surprise to us that most of the artists actually didn't have very utopian or radical wishes for their process. There seemed to be two primary reasons for this. Many of the artists – successful and experienced ones such as Eugenio Barba from Odin Teatret, Richard Lowdon from Forced Entertainment or Elizabeth LeCompte from The Wooster Group – answer that they already feel they can try out anything they want every time they start a new project. They are not harbouring any impossible wishes to change things, and they feel that for years they have had the artistic freedom that allows them to work in the way that they want, including in new ways. The second reason, I think, is that the artists in general are characterized by a very practical and concrete approach to their work. Most of them were simply not particularly interested in the more 'philosophic' aspect of the question that might lead to the wish for something impossible – which was what we were fishing for, to spark off ideas for impossible experiments. They are certainly very interested in realizing dreams and ideas, also very complex and impossible ones, aesthetically, but they are not very interested in utopian processes, rather in concrete and effective processes that will enable them to realize their ideas.

What is striking, however, from an organizational and political perspective is that a recurring 'utopian' wish from the interviewed artists is to have a rehearsal period where all the participants in a production – creative, technical, performing – are present all the time from start to finish, and where you have a rehearsal hall with the same dimensions as the performance space, or even better, where you are able to rehearse and produce in the performance space from start to finish. These two wishes are often expressed with a sigh of longing, because apparently they seem for most of the artists to be an impossible dream. Although from a sober perspective one would think that at least the wish of working with the whole team for the duration of the rehearsal period, as a basic working condition for producing a performance, was a fairly modest one? It would be interesting to do the statistics of how large a percentage of theatre artists in general would prefer those working conditions, and how large a percentage of performances are actually produced under those conditions.

To me one of the most fascinating and mysterious elements that appears in the interview material again and again, is time. Most of the artists talk about time as an essential condition or as an element you struggle with or have to deal with, and a large number of these artists wish for 'more time' for the process. But the more you look at the different statements about time the more mysterious the concept seems to become. Especially the concept of 'more time'. I started wondering if most artists would always think that the product could be even better if they had one more week – or a month – or six months. Simply because they experience the creative process as a continuous development and unfolding that keeps opening new possibilities, new heights, new visions of perfection, and never ends. Is the perfect amount of rehearsal time always what you have – plus one more week? And what would happen if you were suddenly given 'more time' as an unexpected gift? At the exact time of the process where you feel it's missing and the opening is approaching with frightening speed. What exactly would you do with it, how would you use it? Is it always the same specific part of the process that is requiring more time? Is it always the same part of the process that has taken 'too long' in relation to the total amount of time? Is the reality that the final objectives of the process can only be reached in the transition from rehearsal to performance? And maybe the most important question of all: How do you know when you are finished?[4]

Very few of the interviewees express the temporal aspect of the process as something other than just the amount, for example as 'phases'. Eugenio Barba does not indicate exactly how much time he and his performers need to go through the dialectic process from improvisation to fixing to the embodiment that gives life to the expression. He just says that it takes a very long time, longer than any normal person would want to spend on it! But the phases in the process seem to define the time, instead of the other way round. The rehearsal process is finished when you have arrived at the last phase. In that way you could say that Barba is one of the few interviewed artists who does not wish for more time, but on the other hand knows exactly what he wants to do with 'a lot of time'. Other artists have no illusions about utopian wishes for more time: Jan Fabre, for instance, states that the amount of rehearsal time has no influence whatsoever on whether the product will be good or not. It is worth noting, though, that directors such as Jan Fabre, Eugenio Barba, Heiner Goebbels, Elizabeth LeCompte, Richard Lowdon and Wayn Traub are able to work on a project for several months or even years, on and off, whereas other directors such as Annabel Arden and Diane Paulus are familiar with the strict demands of the institutional theatre of opera and musical, for example, where you really have to be, in Arden's words, 'on top of what time there is'. Although she adds, '… mostly, I'd say, there isn't enough time. Mostly I just think it's insane how little time there is.'

Personally, the most important thing that I have learned from these generous, original, intelligent, funny, idealistic and persistent people from all these different fields of performing arts is that they all work in a way that they love. They work in a way that is meaningful and useful for them as artists and persons. They know what makes them good and what they enjoy and they make sure, more or less consciously, that they work under the conditions that make them good. Many of them reflect on how they have learned to deal with for example troublesome collaborators or challenging working conditions – and some have more radical ways of dealing with those than others, these are some of the funniest bits – but they don't fight themselves, they don't pervert themselves to fit into a work method or a system that essentially doesn't suit them or makes it impossible for them to thrive and create. There is no doubt in my mind that that is one of the essential conditions for their success. And it has made me question and revise the way I approach production and rehearsals. For each of us, this material will reflect differently and be striking in different ways. Sometimes the differences and sometimes the similarities will be the most fascinating; sometimes the unique artistic voice stands out, and sometimes the almost universal parallels surprise. To me, each new study brings out new patterns, and I hope that it will continue to inspire other artists, researchers, students and creative professionals of all kinds.[5]

Notes

1 Laboratoriet was based at Entré Scenen from 2005 to 2011 and at the dance venue Bora-Bora from 2011 to 2013. In 2013 Laboratoriet became an independent organization, and in 2016 changed its name to Seachange Lab, www.teaterseachange.dk

2 The total Rehearsal Matters-collection can be found at www.rehearsalmatters.org

3 Bloomsbury's online resource Drama Online can be found at www.dramaonlinelibrary.com

4 The idea of giving an extra week of rehearsal time as a last-minute surprise to a production to see what they would do with it is a wonderful and totally impossible experiment that I still haven't found a way of realizing. But Rehearsal Matters inspired a series of experiments at Laboratoriet from 2011 to 2013 that we called *Utopia*, and one of them, *Utopia 2*, was about the concept of time in a rehearsal process. Documentation from Laboratoriet's experiments can be found at www.teaterseachange.dk or www.seachangelab.dk

5 Parts of this text have been published in Danish in the article 'Fra utopi til metode. Projektet og vidensbanken Rehearsal Matters', *Peripeti* 16 (2011).

Interviews

1

Annabel Arden

Why

How did you end up in theatre?

I got into theatre, I think, as a child, because I remember doing a lot of plays at school. And I was very fortunate, I went to a school where I was really allowed to do what I wanted to do. Nobody ever said, that I can remember, 'Ooh, do you think that's a good choice?' And we had a lot of possibilities to do things by ourselves. I remember I did a poem from *Alice in Wonderland* – 'The Walrus and the Carpenter' – and I remember making oyster costumes for all my friends. I directed that and it was my idea. I also acted in a lot of plays. And then later, we had a swimming pool, which was going to be knocked down, because it was no good anymore. And I asked if I could use it for a piece of theatre before it was knocked down. I wanted to do *Agamemnon* by Aeschylus – I was only about fifteen – and nobody said to me, 'I think that's a bit much.' That was what was amazing about that school. They just said, 'Oh, alright then. If you've got any problems, let us know.' That I remember very strongly because of the space. It was this weird space, an old nineteenth-century swimming pool, so it echoed a lot, and they had those little changing cubicles along the edge of the pool, little doors like for horses, and I just thought it was great. I also made a play in the boiler room of the school, with the pipes and the boilers, a kind of installation, because we were supposed to give the new kids a Halloween party every year. I chose that space because it was dark and scary. And again, nobody said no. So I owe my school a lot, I think. Because I was allowed.

And then I suppose I knew I would do it. Went to university, went to Cambridge. And met up with Simon McBurney. With him, I founded Complicite. Not immediately on leaving Cambridge, but pretty much.

Figure 1 Barbara Simonsen and Annabel Arden, London, May 2010

And do you remember, at school, why you thought theatre was so wonderful, why you had to do it?

I don't remember… I dressed up a lot. I had a big dressing-up box at home. If I think about it now, I think probably it was an escape. I think there were things about my life at home which I wanted to escape from. Nothing very traumatic, but probably I found early on that it was a very good way out of listening or looking at whatever the adults were doing. Just to go into my world. And I read a great deal. I was an insomniac from a very early age, I slept very very little. I still sleep little. And I read, I just read all night.

Can you describe how you and Simon got together?

We met at Cambridge University, which is an odd university for theatre, because there is no theatre course, but a lot of people go there to do theatre. Like at my school, you have a lot of opportunities to just make your own stuff. And unless your work is really terrible people just let you get on with it. So I don't remember doing any academic work at all, really, we just did endless theatre experiments. I became very strong friends with Simon, and we were both looking for something. We saw [Tadeusz] Kantor, who came to this country round about that time, and Comediants, and this sort of thing, and we both discovered that we had a dissatisfaction with a traditionally English career path. Would we end up at the National Theatre, the Royal Shakespeare Theatre? We didn't want to do any of that. And we were fascinated with Europe. I was always interested in European plays, always had been, I don't know why exactly. Except again, thanks to my school I was taught languages very well, and so I could read German and French very easily. And Simon then discovered the Lecoq theatre school in Paris. He was a year older than I, so he went off to Lecoq, and I went to visit him. And it was the most exciting thing I could possibly have imagined. Paris at that time – it was still dirty, you know, that was before they really cleaned it up. It was just amazing. The freedom. The freedom to explore and discover, and the freedom from words. Because we both had very literate, literary upbringings. To be free from that, and to go back…

When I graduated I didn't immediately go to Lecoq, I did another thing with friends I met through Simon: Neil Bartlett, who is a major theatre director now, and a wonderful Latvian woman called Banuta Rubess, who also is a great director. We made a collective. And we actually felt it was appropriate and fine to call it a socialist-feminist collective. It was 1982. We did that for a year, a fantastic, incredible experience. At the end of that year Simon called me and said, 'Shall we just make an experiment?' and I said, 'Yeah, fine, sure…' We made one show, one little show, and it seemed to go terribly well.

Then I took a break and went off to Paris, and began to work with Monika Pagneux and Philippe Gaulier. I did some work at Lecoq, a part of the LEM [Laboratoire d'Étude du Mouvement], but I never did the full two-year course. And Complicite just organically seemed to evolve. We often talked about stopping. But somehow, people seemed to want it, and we wanted it. But even at that early stage we flowed in and out. Simon was always there. There were a few shows I missed, I went in and out. Marcello [Magni], once he came, was there. In the first show there was a woman called Fiona Gordon and she didn't ever do another show with us. In the second show came Jos Houben. I suppose it really took a good ten years of solid work of my life. The last full-time show I did was *Street of Crocodiles* [1992], in which I was performing. But I was often on the outside as a director, although we didn't really split the roles till slightly later on. We did everything. In a sense, it was a collective. It wasn't politically motivated or articulately so, but in essence, it was a collective.

How

Can you describe a typical rehearsal process of Complicite – a basic pattern?

There were certain constants, but they did vary a lot. We would spend some time talking about the idea and the theme. I think Simon was very influenced by Jacques Lecoq and by the final part of the work at the Lecoq school, where you're given a 'command'. Which is essentially a theme. Finding the theme was very important. And sometimes it was easier than others. In the first few shows it was very clear what we wanted to do. I think it got more complex later. Let's take a famous one: *A Minute Too Late* [1984]. That very strongly came from Simon, because he knew he wanted to do a piece about death. He had done his command at Lecoq about his father's death, which was essentially the last scene of that piece where the doctor gives the diagnosis. He always knew he wanted to make a bigger piece from that. So the theme was death. Having decided the theme, we did research – we went to funeral parlours and talked to undertakers, and we went and sat in graveyards and looked at people coming to visit graves. We talked a lot about all the situations related to death, the funeral buffet, being alone in your flat… We'd make a huge list of these and then just try and do them, basically.

We always began the day with some kind of physical work. Play as well, we played a lot. A lot of ball games, a lot of stupid games. We'd make a lot of material, sometimes tiny things, sometimes extended scenes, and then we would try to document them. We tried to write down what we did or at least keep some kind of reasonable note. Because you think you've got it in your head, but at the end of the week you don't know what you've done. We'd stick them up on the wall, those little scraps of paper, and keep collecting objects. Everything was organic at that stage, there were only a few people in that show, and me on the outside. We would invite people, friends, pretty much every week, every few weeks. On Friday afternoon, we'd play little things, to see what would work. And then we'd start to try to find what we called an 'order' – that was to write it. But most of the time was spent creating material. The order was the painful part. Because you have to cut. And then towards the end, it would become clear that certain things were *numbers* in the commedia sense. They were numbers that had to be perfect, otherwise there was no reason to do them. For example the dance that comes out of the church scene in *A Minute Too Late*, where it suddenly goes into a little jazz music and they start to dance, there is *no* excuse for doing that, unless it's perfect. That was also true of the hearse, the scene where Jos [Houben] drives the crazy hearse. Those had to be practised every day.

So there was the creation of material, there was trying to find an order that worked – and sometimes, of course, there are tricky places in the order, where you can't find how one scene develops into the next, so you've got writing problems. And then there was what we called 'roder le spectacle' – you have to really screw it down. To perfect it, practise it. Of course, there was never enough time to practise. Even though we had long rehearsal periods, we had to have a first night, because we had to book to tour. So we would go on working all the way through the tour. I can say that rehearsal never ended. Never. We played *Street of Crocodiles* on and off for about seven years, and we were still rehearsing at the end of it. You have to. Because things die, have to be got rid of or replaced or better ideas come, or actors get replaced.

Things are re-rehearsed and change organically, or the space changes. Your relationship to the material changes. That is the great pleasure of working as we do and did. It's not finished.

And did you find, when you redid A Minute Too Late – *that the rehearsal process had changed in some ways?*

It's always different when you redo something. We redid *A Minute Too Late* many times. Each time there would be different imperatives. For example, somebody was dissatisfied with a thing they'd done and wanted to make it better. Or we couldn't remember bits, had to reinvent bits. It wasn't always videoed. And things changed with the act of remembering. We certainly made the physical environment more sophisticated as we got richer. The first graveyard was literally bricks and breeze blocks that we picked out of the road. Later we'd have more money to actually go and hire or borrow real gravestones. Because we were still in that stage where we thought that it had to be real. Years later, we found designers who actually could make you a gravestone that was good enough to look like a real one. We had different physical ideas, for example if the space changed. Sometimes you had to make it translate into a bigger space, like when we took it to the National Theatre.

The last incarnation of *A Minute Too Late* was twenty years after it was made [2005]. I remember there was a big discussion about what we should change and why. Would it work, and how would we relate to it if we didn't change it? We had to face the fact that it was in some senses a period piece. There were certain things that we would never do, now, were we to make a show about death. And of course, we were much older, the boys were much older, and it was very, very hard. It was quite a moving experience, because they had to confront their mortality in the doing of it. And that's what made it good. Nothing really major was changed. There were certain details. Some of the text was made a little sharper, a little cleaner, but really, mainly, it was as it was. But what was moving was, they were older. And my God, they had to work.

It was really hard. They did it, which was fantastic. We still talk, half-jokingly, about whether we should do *Street of Crocodiles* when we're all sixty. Because that would be about right. And we couldn't. But we would have to find another way of doing it. We also did *Der Besuch der Alten Dame* [*The Visit*, 1989] by Dürrenmatt, where Simon and Kathryn Hunter in their twenties played people who were supposed to be well into their sixties. And I often joke and say, 'Well come on, it's time now!'

Did you find that your own approach to rehearsal process had changed in some basic way?

It's hard to say with that piece, because by that time they really owned it, those three men. And when you're remaking something it's not the same as making something from scratch. But I suppose my process personally has been very influenced by the fact that since 1993 I've done much less devising work than I did before, because my own personal work has moved away from Complicite into opera, into texts. I think I've retained from Complicite the need to play. We play before we actually do the thing. As much as you can. It's quite difficult in opera to do it. I've had to adapt because of the specific demands that singers have. But the great thing is that I can bring the idea of physical invention – the idea that we can make it what we want it to be – into the opera world. So that there isn't a set way, you have to devise it, and you have to make it work as a routine. You have to practise, physically, which is something they are not so familiar with. They say, 'No no, we've done it.' And I say, 'Well, it's not good enough. It's not as good as your singing. Your singing is very good. The action is not very good.' And that's a battle. They think they've done it. And you go, no, but the quality – the quality – this is the key word. The quality of how you pick that prop up, how you touch her… That's hard. It depends on you either having a very willing young company and a lot of time, or very great stars. All the people in between: it's extremely difficult. Because they're operating in a highly constrained atmosphere and they have little time.

They have very high expectations on a very small technical part of their being. It's not their fault! But you have to go for it.

In terms of my process, I suppose you're more able as you get older to say, 'What is the result I have to achieve?' – and to work backwards from that. What process must we then go through? You can be more confident about certain things, I would say. But then again, I haven't done any devising from nothing for a long time. And that's a special process. The closest to devising I have done recently, was *Heldenplatz* [2010] by Thomas Bernhard that I co-directed with Annie Castledine. You could say it has got nothing to do with devising because it's a really big, long text. But it was absolutely not clear how to do it. Bernhardt's work is these short little lines. There's no punctuation. Some of the action's clear, but you could do it in a million ways. And there I found that my process had changed, because it's more linked to really exploring text. Not just for meaning, but for sound, rhythm, music. So I find it an interesting journey that I came from Complicite into opera and now I'm very interested in these texts, which in fact are really musical. It's a question of trying to find the shapes and make the actors see the shapes and the value of repetition. There was a lot of repetition in that text. Taking it away from an actor-led psychology to determine the action – instead, the action is a musical action and corresponds to the architecture of the text. Poetic matrix of the text. I'm interested in finding that, and there are so many processes. Sometimes we would just speak it and speak it. And then I would see it in my mind's eye and say to the actor, 'Okay, try this action here, this action here. Do you see the vocabulary now, can you invent now?' If they see it then they invent. But that's different from the ensemble writing it. For me that's the significant difference about Complicite. And I think to a certain extent it's still true, although it's changed as well. But there, we had to write the show. There was no show.

But even when you are doing a play by Shakespeare, on some level it still is true. If the work is going to be good, the actors must possess it. If they don't possess it, it's never what it could be. Never. So you have to find ways so that they possess. The first thing for me is that they have to be made into a company. And that takes time. They are individuals, they have come from very different places, different preoccupations. It's absolutely essential that they become a company.

And for that you use the games?

The first and the most important thing is that everybody has to be there every day. It's totally irrelevant whether they are in a scene or not. They are essential to be there. And that can be difficult. With *Heldenplatz* it was very difficult. Partly, we had no money, and there's a scene at the end where suddenly five people come that you haven't seen before. They are actually crucial. So were we going to pay them for the whole time, when they are in a third of it and they have maybe one line each? Very difficult. The theatre had no money. We had to compromise. And it made huge difficulties for us. We only got there just by the skin of our teeth. And only because they were very, very willing people. But you could feel it wasn't right. And also, we wasted all that creative talent. It would have helped a lot to have them there all the time. They would have seen things, they'd have taken the burden away, because the first scene of that play is two people for forty-five minutes, and only one of them speaks. The other has a huge silent role. It's an enormous thing. So to actually have the creative crucible of a company would have been very nice. Didn't have it.

When you are able to have everybody, do you then spend a lot of time talking?

No, no, no. I try to talk as little as possible. As *little* as possible. It should be self-evident. We do a lot of physical work, we sing, we play games. If there are specific physical demands from the piece then you have to work on them from day one. If you know you're going to do a dance, you start to dance. If you know there's going to be a fight, or you know there is going to be an enormous change of landscape, you have to start working on this vocabulary from the very, very beginning. And sometimes you get everybody to play a scene. Everybody gets to be the king. Or the king is amplified by a huge body, or… There are many many ways.

Do you also design the games so that they will get them in the direction that you want?

Yes. And you hope that you'll discover some new ones, because it's fatal to always do the same thing, it has to be different every time. I think that's really important. I said we didn't talk, but there have been some rehearsal periods in Complicite where we did talk a lot. But it was as a result of the work. As time has gone on, we've spent more time talking, I think, particularly in the shows, which took their inspiration from quite a lot of text. The stories of Murakami [*The Elephant Vanishes*, 2003] or *Mnemonic* [1999], which was based on quite a complex book about the discovery of the Tyrol Ice Man in the snow. It took a collective work to absolutely get into the text. There was a lot of photocopying of pages and chopping them up with scissors and regluing them together and reading them out differently and acting them – basically, making a script. That happened a little bit with Bruno Schulz's *Street of Crocodiles* as well. I think you have to try to engage the actor on all the levels. Emotional, intellectual, physical of course, sexual. That's the skill of the director, guiding, leading, pushing. Very often – and Simon is really brilliant at this – people find things at different speeds. You'll have some actors who are very quick, who'll find loads of stuff themselves to do. Some actors who are very slow, who appear not to be finding anything. They are, of course, but it's slow and it's subterranean, and they get worried and upset, because they haven't got anything to do and everybody else is doing stuff. Then you have to manage that – you may help them find things, but that can also not work, because it's like grafting on and not really organic – it can be very complicated.

But the most fun rehearsal periods were basically characterized by chaos. Fantastic amounts of chaos. Just fantastic. And risk and fear and fun and nobody really knew – *nobody* knew what the show was going to look like. We knew we had good bits!

In my early opera work, I was closer to that world, so I allowed there to be a lot of chaos. And people found this really, really frightening. Very difficult. I sailed very close to the wind early on, and I just managed to get away with it. But as you work more and more with opera and music, I think your preoccupation changes. Because the chaos is really hard for singers. The brain doesn't work in the same way. If you have to reproduce a score with the most terrifying accuracy, there comes a point in the rehearsal process where they *cannot* reimprovise and rechange action, because there is too much musical work to do. I didn't understand that for a long time. I thought they were being frightened and rigid. But it's not that at all. And I had to work with some really great singers to understand it. Singers who would say, 'It's fine – I don't mind changing, I don't mind changing, it's fine, it's fine…' Alessandro Corbelli, who is the greatest buffo baritone in the world, he's incredibly funny, it's like working with all the Marx Brothers rolled into one – and he is a brilliant singer. He would go very far in changing things, and then there would come a rehearsal where I'd see him get a little bit… And I'd say, 'Alessandro? How are you, what's going on?' and he'd say, 'Hmmm. I think we should fix it like it is.' And I'd say, 'Yes. I think you're right.' [*Laughs.*] Or I would say to him, 'There is that one thing where I'm not sure, I think we could find something better', and he'd say, 'Yes, but I've learned it now, and that's a tricky passage for my voice.' So I thought, okay, if *you're* saying that… 'I don't mind changing', he said, 'but you have to understand, I'll have to rethink my phrasing and I'll have to rethink my breathing, and I haven't got time.'

It's interesting. I've learned an awful lot about music. You begin to find out what the music is really doing, and where your limits of chaos are. And of course, it also depends on the composer. Partly he was saying that because he had tricky little da capo Donizetti aria which is like a machine. He sang *Gianni Schicchi* [2004] with me, and that piece of Puccini is a precision instrument. It's like commedia in that sense. It *is* commedia. And you can change things, but you need time.

As you get older, I think you understand more and more that the real work happens on a deeply human level, between yourself as a director and the performer. That you really have to listen. You really have to try and draw out whatever is there in your performers. You don't impose, and play, and reconstruct all your ideas and so on – we were more like that with each other when we were younger. Now, particularly since I don't perform in the shows I'm directing, it's a very different work. To release the creativity of the people who've got to carry it.

I think it is very interesting what you said about how now you tend to know what you want and then work your way backwards, how do I get there – but in the beginning, when we start doing this work we don't know where we're going. It's a different approach. And maybe it's a strange question, but I wonder which one is better? Or is it just the natural result of getting older?

I think you have to try to put yourself in situations, as you get older, where you don't know where you're going. I think if you lose the capacity to set out on a journey which is really scary, because you have no idea whether it's going to work or not, and you really don't know what the end result will look like... If you can bear to keep doing that all your life, that's where you stay young, creatively, I think. Because the other skills will always be growing anyway. But I think you do lose a sense of freedom. Sometimes it's very hard, because you're playing for bigger stakes. There may be more money involved. People's lives are more precarious, people's reputations – not that that should ever matter. And sometimes just the fact that there are much bigger theatres involved. Not that it's anything to do with prestige, just with the fact that the space is very big. It has to be negotiated with more forethought. If you're playing to very large audiences, that's a technique and it has to be built into the process. But I think Peter Brook was very brilliant in that he always made his new creations in the same place. He has that perfect space, where he understands its dynamic very well. I don't know that I'm right, he might have made some shows not in the Bouffes Du Nord, but I think pretty much they were all made there. Then of course they went to other places and they grew or they shrank or whatever, but he knew where he started from. We never had that luxury.

The essential

Looking back at all the rehearsal processes, what do you think is really the essential condition or the essential thing that makes a good rehearsal process?

The people. The team. Casting. If you've got an amazing group of people and you've somehow sniffed out the right kinds of chemistries so there is some kind of amazing charge, humanly, nothing can go wrong. It doesn't matter what else goes wrong. Lots of things are going to go wrong. That's number one. You have to have the people. The second is the space. You can have the right people, and if you are rehearsing in a space that kills you, you're constantly fighting. Every day the space is killing you on some level. There are spaces that kill. Or spaces that put a difficulty again and again. It's a vibration. It's not just to do with walls and light, sometimes you have a simple physical difficulty which you have to fight against. But usually that can be solved, even if it's annoying. Like pillars, or cold. But the spatial things will influence and determine something about that piece. Again, if the people are alive enough it'll be fine.

The third is time. Sometimes you can do fantastic work really fast. I'm not saying it has to be long. But you have to know how to use the time. You have to be on top of what time there is. And mostly, I'd say, there isn't enough time. Mostly I just think it's insane how little time there is. There used to be a lot of time, in the great golden period of ensemble-created opera, post-war in Germany, and even in England when they started the English National Opera Company, there was more time: a) because there were fixed ensembles, so people knew each other, so a lot of time was saved and b) people would work on roles with their directors and their conductors for years, with a production in mind, so they would know they were going to sing this work or that. And they'd have long detailed informative sessions; as they are learning the music they are also thinking creatively with the director. That is really hard to get now. But all forms need time, it's a lie to say that they don't. All the forms need time. Think how much time dancers take, how long it takes to make one minute of really good choreography. It takes forever. Today I'm afraid our culture is very poor at recognizing this. Particularly in this country. People think you're being indulgent, and that the purchase of time is not really a good investment.

Can you say more about what is the right cast, what is the charge, what does it consist of?

There are a couple of things that I have noticed. You need a degree of homogeneity. You need enough that's shared. They don't all have to have the same background, or the same training, but if there are too many really disparate elements it's tricky, because it's harder to bind it. I had a cast, for example, who were all wonderful, but they were split between Italian singers, English singers and Russian singers. It was like trying to get mice back into a cage. Because they all had such different temperaments, different needs in how to work. The Italians had to have fun, the English singers really wanted to work it out, and the Russian singers needed a fight. That sounds xenophobic, but it's not, it's true! That was tricky. It would have been great, if there had been just one culture that was dominant. Then you could have the spice of an extra Russian and the rigour of a nice English singer and it would have all hung together better. So a degree of homogeneity is actually essential. In Complicite we would interpret it in the way that we had to have enough people who knew what the chorus work really was, really, truly – then you could have a few actors with outstanding qualities, extraordinary qualities, who didn't know that work. Because they would be carried by the body, and they'll integrate into the body.

So you're trying to create a body, like a real, living organism. You can't graft the head of a pig, and the legs of a cow… It won't function. But you want it to be a surprising body, a body of many many talents – so the basic tissue has to knit together. Then you do want really surprising people. Some of this, some of that. And, it's very important to have an element of conflict. If everyone gets on too well, and they all know each other, and they know each other's children, and they go and have Sunday lunch, that's never going to work. If possible, you want some serious sexual attraction – best of all possible worlds, that isn't going to end in disaster – but you have to risk. But they all have to have one thing, which is essentially that they place a higher value on the work itself than themselves. If you have one ego in there, it's a pain in the ass. For me they all have to be people who are coming from that place. It's not about me, it's about us, it's about the work, it's about the writer etc. And if you've got that openness, there you go.

Even the most peculiar casts can be knitted together. You don't always know when you cast people, then you put them together as a group and you go, oops! Actually, an important part of the process in Complicite was that for us the rehearsal didn't start on day one of rehearsal. We had many pre-periods. This is very important. That you have a kind of workshop period, where you're working directly on or towards your material with people who may or may not end up in the cast. And you look at groups of people together. So that when you're finally trying to decide who you're going to ask, you don't see individual, individual, individual. You remember a good combination there, and that it was wonderful when she came in because then he had someone to play with, and so on. You start to compose from nuclei, instead of just so-and-so for this role, so-and-so for this role.

I do it sometimes with opera, but there I have much less control over which singers I ultimately use. Horrible. But there are certain patches of certain operas where I'll work with actors before I see the singers. If I *can* work with some singers it's better, but often I can't. Or I won't be working with the ultimate singer I'm working with, but with some singer. So that I can begin to understand more fully the real playing dynamics before I hit day one of rehearsal. And often in opera I have to be able to play it myself. It's the quickest way. Therefore, I have to know the music very very well. I find that very difficult, to actually memorize music.

Problems

What is the biggest difficulty or problem in the rehearsal period?

I don't know really. There are so many things that can happen in a rehearsal period, and so many variables, you never really know. People can reveal themselves to be very different than you thought they were. The material can refuse to yield. I think really, in order to be able to cope with everything, you need to maintain your confidence as a director. You somehow have to not be in a state of fear. It's as simple as that, really. It helps if you're extremely well prepared on some level. And if you're devising from nothing, how can that be? You can have prepared, you can have thought around, and you can have put systems in place, whereby you have a lot of other people thinking around: a designer who's coming in constantly with input, or flexibility with your producers who understand the process, who know very well that they might have to cancel a preview or two. In that sense that's preparing, because it's bolstering your sense of everybody understanding the reality of where you are. You have to maintain a certain distance, emotional distance. If you get too emotionally identified with the project, it's not good. You have to be identified and not identified – simultaneously. If possible, you have completely sorted your emotional and domestic life out, and it's not there. It no longer exists. I had a wonderful rehearsal period in Texas for five weeks. Because I couldn't get on a plane and get back to my family. Too far, you know. Paris, more difficult – you *could*…

So no distractions. Confidence, no distractions, and a lot of energy. Physically I think you have to approach it as if you're climbing Mount Everest. You do need to be in a physical state when you can give everything every day. I had a nice experience in Australia where I was directing a play by my husband Stephen Jeffreys [*The Art of War*, 2007]. The Sydney Theatre Company had commissioned him to write a new play and me to direct it. It was very experimental in form. Very experimental. It was for an ensemble of twelve actors and I made them do a lot of physical, which they weren't used to. Some of them were not young. They were fantastic actors, but the forms were so different and experimental for them. It had many narrative threads, and we had all sorts of stuff where we had to use real guns, which were decommissioned of course, but we had to really use them – strip them and put them back together again like soldiers do. They couldn't believe, these actors, that I just kept going. That I was in there an hour before them and I was there an hour after them, and I just never, never flagged. I thought, what are you talking about? That's what you do! And I realized that this was the old Complicite training. Because before the days when we had to worry about actually how much we paid people or whether we belonged to any union, we would just get there, and we wouldn't go home until we thought we'd done enough for the day. And that could be anything. We didn't stop to eat until somebody, usually Marcello because he is a good Italian, would say, 'I'm gonna die – I have to eat *now*.' Then we would stop. There was never this 'ten till one, two till five'. No. We were just in there. I'm very, very grateful I had it. Because that's how I am in a rehearsal. Somebody has to come and point to a watch and say, *'It's time! Stop!'*

The damaging thing about opera is that is that it's so blocked in time. There is not one minute that you can go over. It's simply not allowed. It's very damaging, and you have to not let it damage you. You have to stay in an open state and at ten o'clock, you have to say to everybody in the room, 'Now look, today we're doing such and such a scene, and I really hope that it's going to be so exciting that when we get to one o'clock – *if*, *just* by going on for five minutes we might *just* get there – will you be ready for that, is everybody in the room willing? It probably won't happen, but you never know, we might be very good.' That's what you learn in opera. To not conform in your soul. It's such a conformist milieu, it's unbelievable, but you just have to make sure you don't.

So there are all the external possible problems of time and space and there is the director's inner dangers of falling into the fear, falling into the no-confidence and so on. But do you also find that there is something in a rehearsal process – I mean in the way that you work – something innate or inherent in the process, a barrier that you will bump into every time, and there is nothing to be done about it, it's something that you just have to overcome every time?

I don't know. I think… I don't know the show that I've done where I haven't had a week where it feels like nothing's going right and nothing's happening. Where somehow it fails to progress. It just seems to be static. And all your ideas look terrible. You feel you are losing time and so on. And I think it's to be avoided. I think you have to choose new strategies every time for avoiding it, but what it is, I think, is… It's somehow not being flexible enough to keep the life in the room at all times. If it becomes routine in some way – so people go, 'Oh right, that's how we're working.' And they're quick to do that, performers. They are like children, you know. Something switches off. So at the risk of upsetting people, I think you have to surprise – come from different angles, challenge. I think a lot of directors do this instinctively. I think it is an instinct. If you're too concerned about being kind, you kill that instinct. I'm not very good at having fights. But I actually think it's part of it. Really challenging people. You have to keep challenging people, and challenging yourself, of course – but you have to risk conflict. And that's why the theatre is so fantastic, because people working in it, I hope, will always understand that the conflict is a creative conflict, it's not personal, it's not racist, it's not this or that. It's not like an office. You can't issue me with a warning for being nasty to you – because this is a rehearsal room. And it doesn't matter how nasty I am, actually. I mean, unless the behaviour is absolutely extreme. I can go pretty far, if you're my actor – because I'm doing it for you. For the show. And God forbid that there should come a time when that's not allowed.

As I say, I'm not very good at these conflicts, so it doesn't happen to me, but yes, people do behave outrageously in theatre. And I think unless they're just completely horrible people, it's simply an instinct for how to keep the electricity in the room. It's got to be there. Or it's got to be just hovering on the edge. Sometimes you also need calm, steady rhythm where people are learning and you make an atmosphere of real trust. Where they take the time to learn to map, to see their way through the show, to feel supported, to feel open. But if they're so supported and they're so listened to, then it goes thhhhh... And you can't get the energy back. That's really a danger. And you can't get the discipline back. So it has to be high discipline, high demand, within a safe humane framework. So they know that you are not a dictator, you're not a nut. But you know, many great directors are great dictators. And the actor needs that. How can you push yourself to climb these terrible mountains? You need somebody thrashing you from behind, on some level, or you wouldn't do the work. There is a basic laziness which infects a huge majority of performers. That's the charm. You have all this talent and it won't work. No, I'm joking, but it's part of the director's function. They're frightened, you see. The main problem is fear. I think it is *the* biggest problem. That people who are very talented live with a great deal of fear. And they find all sorts of ways of dealing with it. One of the things that scares them the most is achieving more than they have ever achieved. Of being so startlingly extraordinary. They're terrified of it on one level – because can they ever do it again? Will they hold on to it? What will happen? That's all. They like to stay where they know.

Dreams

Is there anything that you would like to change in the rehearsal process, either in the structure of it, or maybe in the ingredients, the place, the people? If you could change or try out anything?

Well, I certainly think if you're talking about opera, it would be wonderful to have a kind of regular atelier of good singers who are really prepared to give time and thought and creativity without the pressure of a performance. That we would do it for ourselves. Not simply because we're paid to do it and there's a contract. And if that could be created around a company or a production – that would be great.

And another thing I've often fantasized about: There's a wonderful film called *Vanya on 42nd Street* – and as I understand it, Louis Malle or Wally Shawn collected those actors, or they collected themselves. They met in each other's houses for a period of *years* before they made that film. Just to explore the text. A very slow, very relaxed approach. It was more or less the same collection of people, and that's why it took years, because there were very few times that they could all be free. So they inhabited those characters in a very, very from the inside-out way. And I'd love to do an experiment like that. To really take a long time over something. So it has to be worth it. You've got to take a text that is sufficiently subtle. That will reveal and reveal and reveal to you. But I'm sure that would be good.

And then, for me it's very rare that I have a rehearsal room that I really like. Often it's a problem that you need to rehearse with the set. And if the set is for a very large theatre, of course you do have a very large rehearsal room, but the set takes up the whole space. So there's no flat, empty, neutral… I would like in my work to have all the physical stuff we need, and another room next door that is perfect, clean, nothing, warm… Clean, that's the other thing. *Only* in Japan have I worked in real, pristine cleanliness. A thing of beauty, an aesthetic value in itself. I think that's very important. The aesthetic value is everything. I'd work in Japanese conditions – that's what I'd like.

Interview: Barbara Simonsen

Annabel Arden (UK)

Annabel Arden (born 1959) is a director, actress and co-founder of the company Complicite in 1983. Her career as an independent director encompasses theatre, opera and broadcasting as well as devising new work. She has directed for Opera North, The English National Opera, The Royal National Theatre, Almeida Theatre and BBC.

Select works

A Minute Too Late (1985, 2005)
The Winter's Tale (1991)
La Bohème (2012)
Café Kafka (2014)

Website

www.complicite.org

2

Eugenio Barba

Why

Why did you choose to work with theatre?

I chose theatre to be able to put on a mask. It made me an 'artist' and therefore I could escape the way I was treated in Oslo (it was in the late 1950s) as a dark-skinned migrant worker.

How

How much has the way you work with performances and rehearsal processes changed over the years?

It has changed radically. I would say that today I am doing almost the opposite of what I did in the beginning. Furthermore, a good deal of the taboos that existed before are now used intentionally to produce new and unfamiliar working situations. Because the main characteristics of Odin Teatret – which is something unique, I think, in European theatre history for the last two hundred years – is that the same core of people have been working together here for more than forty years. Those we call 'the younger ones' have been here for more than twenty years. This means that we know each other very, very well, and obviously that is a great advantage, because it means that all the actors are able to embody part of these experiences – finding personal ways of expression, but within a certain horizon of expression. One might call it a style that enables you to instantly recognize an Odin actor or an Odin performance.

But on the other hand, what I claim is the ghost that scares us to death, is the fear that this knowledge, who we are, the professional identity, becomes mannerism. So how can we fight, every time we begin a new performance, to get as far away as possible from what comes natural to us, the spontaneous, the conditioned reflexes that we have become a part of? Therefore, the biggest task that I and all the actors feel we need to accomplish is to find starting points that are different, and that force us to use all of our experience in a way that is not automatic.

The biggest change is this: When I started making performances I had a text in which the writer had already established the narrative structure. There are characters. When you read this text you know what these characters say, who they are, where they come from, and where they are going. There is a very clear thread, a continuity that enables you to follow it, and you just need to turn these words on paper into human reactions and moods. They must fill the space, they must make a sensual impression so that the spectator becomes conscious of them. But after about ten years we started to move away from that basis, and we started building themes of our own. Instead of having a play that already contained all of the narrative structure we started choosing a theme. For example the meeting between the European immigrants and the local American population. And of course, this is a huge, general issue that one needs to slowly boil down to a number of specific situations. Very concrete situations, with characters that the actors feel they can work with during the rehearsal process, feel inspired by, know how to give life to, fill with nuances – dynamically, emotionally, soundwise, vocally, and also textual. Because we also start finding the texts ourselves, either by using quotations, books, or by writing it ourselves. This is a typical work process that was characteristic of all the travelling theatre companies in the history of the theatre, that is, those that did not present plays by writers. The main part of the travelling theatre companies rehearsed and worked in a way where the actors were also co-writers and had the ability to write scenarios that were changed from location to location.

This was also characteristic of Odin Teatret's way of working in the early 1970s. But still, we had a starting point, a theme. It could be the biography of Dostoyevsky. From his life we could choose certain events as our focus points. How he went from being a young political, intellectual writer who was sentenced to death by the tsar, sent to Siberia, experienced the homage of the dead; later became a kind of reactionary, a great admirer of the tsar and the whole Pan-Slavic ideology. In his works there is a kind of radicalism, a kind of revolutionary, rebellious spirit that caused his novels to be banned in the Soviet Union during the worst periods of Stalinism. That is what you might focus on. We made this performance [*My Father's House*, 1972] right after 1968, so it was also a reflection of the role of the intellectual. But during the years this starting point changed, and I feel it becomes more and more exciting that the outlook I am narrating through the performance or through the actions of the actors is not just one story, but several stories. That means that when I begin a new performance I have several starting points that are not connected with each other.

It started in the 1980s, with a performance called *The Gospel According to Oxyrhincus* [1985]. Here I chose six characters. With a kind of arrogance, I thought that since these characters have very obvious, association-inspiring names, if I change the title of the performance people will think that I am making a performance about them. The six characters were Joan of Arc, Antigone and her brother Polynices, Dostoyevsky's Grand Inquisitor, and a Jew named Zusha Mal'ak from Chassidim. And then there was the false Messiah – Sabbatai Zevi – a Jew from the seventeenth century who was believed by many Jews to be the new Messiah. He lived in Thessaloniki that was under Turkish rule. After a few years where he had made a lot of European Jews move to Palestine the sultan got a bit annoyed with this man and said, either you convert to Islam or you will lose your head. And this Messiah was a very sensible person, so he converted to Islam. But it became another proof that he was Messiah, because he could do anything.

These six people tell the story called *The Gospel According to Oxyrhincus* – about the rebellion that is buried alive, one of the stories from Antigone, and the story of this Jew seeking Messiah in a country where Messiah has already come. But in reality this is a biography of Stalin. So within the same space, without the spectator knowing it,

I am telling two different stories. Some actors are telling one story, other actors are telling another story. Because of the proximity in the space, people think that there is a relation, but there is none. So on a narrative level one is a little confused about what is going on, but organically – that is, in everything that has to do with live relations, dynamic relations, movement and rhythm – there is an abundance of crossroads. So one has a sense that there is a kind of cohesion after all, a sensual, dynamic cohesion. These aspects of the work emerge more and more, and I get a clear understanding of the performance as a living organism. I experience that this living organism consists of various levels of organization as in biology. The first level is in the cells, enabling an organism to live, if the cells are working, and that is what I call presence. The actors must be present. That means they must have an ability to sensually convince the spectators' nervous system that what they are doing corresponds to a human experience, relating to movement, action or intention. So that it is not something abstract or a cliché that does not resonate with the spectators. Once you have built this, you already have a structure that will work as a performance.

For example, dance is a form of performance that is very weak on the narrative level. It has almost no narrative, but still, organically, it has a dramaturgy. With dramaturgy I mean a sequence of actions, and these actions can be of a dynamic, organic kind, or they can be of a narrative kind. If, for instance, we have a young man who has visited Delphi and meets an old man on the way, and the old man says something and the young man kills him – then we have a sequence of actions, and they are of a narrative kind.

So in the first work process you have the text as a starting point and the performance is an interpretation, whereas in the second work process texts and stories become more of a platform on which the drama is played on another level?

Precisely. Before, I started from the narrative to build the dynamic or organic. Now we start from the organic. The actors bring me lots of material, improvisations that they have fixed, songs that they find interesting, texts that they want to narrate – even though they still do not know what we will be narrating. Then we start to build a kind of sequence of scenes and actions that begin to 'suggest' something to us through the dynamics and rhythm, the use of the space, the use of props. We don't understand what it is, but it awakens associations, meanings.

And there they don't even have the characters as they did in The Gospel According to Oxyrhincus*?*

No, exactly. In *The Gospel of Oxyrhincus* they had them, but in other performances, for example in *Kaosmos* [1993], they did not know until the end who they were. After months of rehearsal. Some of them couldn't cope with it, so I gave them a character. Because they could no longer see what they were doing and what they were reacting to. Others could do it. Actors are very different in that respect.

But what I have found most exciting for the last ten years is not just to have these various starting points or themes. Sometimes the themes are not just narrative. One of them was how to tell the story of the fall of communism. It's a good question, but in theatre you have to boil it down to a totally concrete task for the actors. We boiled it down to a ghost wandering through Europe, the ghost of communism, after 1991 and the dissolution of the Soviet Union. I saw communism as a ghost trying to come in, seeking asylum, but nobody wants him in, and he is accompanied by thousands of women in black. Those who have lost sons, brothers, husbands in the Gulag. They are singing a poem by Anna Akhmatova, the Russian poet, an incredibly beautiful poem, 'Requiem', to her son who was taken by the secret police and sent to the Gulag.

At the same time, there is the other theme. How everything that communism was, a dream, a longing for justice, for a society that was built on equality for all – how this ideal or this dream in reality became a crime of gigantic proportions, and how many people fought for communism and became accomplices to the crime without knowing it. How can you express all that too? It was also boiled down to a concrete action: An instrument, a small accordion that plays the *Internationale* by itself, is stabbed by knives and stops playing.

All this begins as a reaction to what goes on around me. Almost all the themes or starting points I have taken have a lot to do with history around me. They are of course questions that are themselves so abstract that they will never work as a performance. It is necessary to turn them into something concrete. Like when you give an actor a task: How do you kill a song? By singing it out of tune or by the singer being killed? They make many different suggestions, and it is very important that the actors have been trained to think and act paradoxically. To act paradoxically is what characterizes the essential artistic process. It is paradoxical to take reality that is three-dimensional and put it onto a canvas that is two-dimensional. It is completely paradoxical. A paradox. Similarly, we take live reactions – love, sex, violence, pain, everything that our bodies suffer or burn for – and transform into conceptual signs that we put on paper. Just as paradoxical. And yet, when people read it – also a conceptual process – suddenly they start to sense it. The only art form in which the paradoxical has become diminished and which is almost a direct reflection of what we see around us in real life is theatre. That is because the essential performance form of our time is no longer theatre, but film and television. And film and television cannot cope with paradoxical or formalized acting styles. Imagine seeing a story about AIDS or rape played as Noh theatre or classical ballet. You have to use a more recognizable, direct physical expression. Which is the convention of everyday behaviour. That has been, unfortunately, the situation for the theatre. Before it was very formalized and stylized, but after Ibsen, Strindberg, Chekhov and Pirandello and all the other writers who presented a whole new world of themes, it is impossible to hold on to the exaggerated style of acting. The choice is either between the old and stylized or the new everyday convention. But no one has been able to find a third possibility, that is, keeping the paradoxical, independent artistic expression, which is theatrical, but created by the actors themselves.

Formalization means that everybody must play something in the same way. Classical ballet, mime, all in the same way. But the paradoxical is like a Lvov painter or an impressionist. There are principles, which say that you must present your impression, you must use the colours and the brush in a certain way, use gestures on the canvas. Those are just principles. But there are no rules. Odin Teatret is not avant-garde or experimental. The experience of Odin Teatret is interesting, because we have found the third way. We are very formalized in our style of acting, but at the same time you cannot call it a continuation of classical ballet, mime, pantomime and so on. When we make a performance we are interested in finding very personal answers to questions that may seem very grand, very sublime. For example the ghost of communism seeking asylum, and no one wants to open their borders to it. But they may also be questions of a different type. Just before the year 2000 a kind of hysteria about the new millennium emerged. We were adjusting clocks all over the world. We talked about how there were 400 days left, 300 days… Would it be different? Would there be a change? Everywhere we went with Odin Teatret, we felt this strange, almost fever-like attitude towards this date. And then I asked myself, will there be a change in the way we think? And the thought turned into: will we also have myths in the new millennium? I started asking that question everywhere I went. The myth of the revolution, of changing the world, has been characteristic of the twentieth century. Whether it was the Fascists, the Nazis, the Bolsheviks, the Christians, or those who weren't Christians. Everybody felt the need to change the world and their fellow humans. Would the same thing happen in the twenty-first century?

I thought that the myth of the revolution would no longer survive, or only as a kind of criminal figure. Just as Medea has survived in our time. Horrible lady who murders her children. Or Oedipus. Or Daedalus, who is also responsible for the death of his son. When you think of Agamemnon, Clytemnestra, all the figures of Greek tragedy – they are all criminals. One big gang! We were never meant to play them on our stages, we were just supposed to condemn them. But they tell us something. So the last revolutionary, who is a Brazilian soldier in the performance *Mythos* [2000], is walking his long after-death passage to reach all these characters from the Greek myths so that he can become one of them.

As you can see, the themes are often incredibly paradoxical, but it is very exciting to make them stimulate both me, the director, and the actors, because not all the actors have the same interests or the same obsession with history. So the trick is to find either characters, or work processes or tasks that stimulate them. And at the same time give the body a sense that it has the chance to expand – even minimally – its range of experience. It is the opposite of taking the three-dimensional reality and placing it on the canvas where it becomes abstract. Here I think in the abstract, the ghost of communism, and then I take it to the concrete. But how do I do it? Take an actor and dress him up? The tragedy, or the terrible fate for us theatre people, is that when you show something on stage, it is always literal. One must show both the literal so that you can recognize it – a person, blond, nice – and at the same time create a kind of hallucination so that suddenly you start not to see this person, but something called Hamlet. And after a while you no longer see a Hamlet, but a person who is actually capable of making you have a dialogue with yourself. About your own life. So there are these three steps that you must employ. Through a kind of technique which in itself is incredibly simple, because it is incredibly concrete, and it must be like a caress. When you receive a caress you don't feel it if it is too weak – and if it is too strong it might hurt. So how do you caress the senses of the audience, and also their memory? That is the basis. Memory is what makes me feel a resonance in my own biography from what I see. It is also very important always to have in mind that I need this performance to speak individual languages, to whisper to anyone, even though they are so different because they have such different human experiences.

What I truly love is to make performances where I don't know what I am saying or what I have wanted to say until the end of the process. That was the case with *Andersen's Dream* [2004], for instance. We started off with various themes, one of them the slave routes. I happened to read that UNESCO had named the year 2000 International Year for the Remembrance of the Slave Trade, and that the slave routes, which are in reality a horrible, degrading event in the history of man, are nevertheless routes where culture has crystallized into syncretism and many new forms of expressions. Just think how many people died to build the pyramids that everyone today is travelling to see.

I explained this theme to the actors, and they looked at me and had never heard of it and thought it was very interesting, but wanted to know concretely, 'What is my role? What am I going to do?' And then I thought that it was interesting how everybody is very concerned and conscious about the physical changes that come with age. Especially the actors who used to be very vital and were able to do a lot of things that they cannot anymore. I suggested that we should also add age as a theme, and that we should go work at a retirement home for a period of time. 'Sure, sure', they said – of course – they always say sure, and then they do what they want! But that was also very abstract, because what would that give them? Is the thing missing that in the end is the absolute essential, the entire anecdote? Or a kind of tension, drama, opposition that is required for both the actor and director to start having ideas and thoughts about how to express it?

But then we also decided to use Hans Christian Andersen. And not until the end did we realize what the whole thing was about. By chance we found a text by Andersen in his diaries, where he says, 'Last night I had a dream that the king had invited me onto his royal ship, and I had to hurry, I started running, running through a forest, I got lost, and it was terrible, but finally I arrived, and then the royal ship had already sailed. Then there was another ship and a skipper who said, "Come, come on board," so I went on board. But when I did, I was pushed downstairs, and I realized that I had come on board a slave ship.' Imagine! After months of work there comes my assistant one day and says, 'Look what I've found in his diary.' That's when the performance started to take shape. It has to do with choosing subconsciously, it has to do with serendipity – the art of finding what you are not looking for. But in order to do that you need large amounts of material. For this performance the actors had more than twenty-four hours of material. We worked for a very long time and everything was cut down to eighty minutes.

Now we are working on a new performance. And to avoid this I say, 'No, you don't have to prepare anything, just be there.' Everybody looks at me in surprise. It's a very long time ago that I have told them to come unprepared. One of the taboos that we used to have was that you could not use material that had been used before. Today we use things again and change them, for example ironically or otherwise. Another taboo was that when you started working on something you would isolate yourself completely from all other tasks and focus only on the performance. Today we will work for a week, then break to go on tour, come back, do an event, rehearse for another week and so on. That kind of fragmentation used to be unthinkable. But again, these are older people with an enormous amount of experience, so all this is a way for us not to repeat the same conditions. A work process must contain an insecurity.

Have you planned other completely new rules or new approaches for the coming performance?

No, the rules are created as you go along. When we start a new performance it is always very important for me to address everything in the actor's expression that communicates with the right side of the brain, which is everything that has to do with singing and movement. The left side is concerned with concepts. Therefore, music is very important. But this time the process began in an entirely different and surprising way. One of the actors had to be singing at all times. When one of them stopped, another one had to begin. That became one of the rules that we had never thought of before. We usually hear one song and evaluate it. This was much more random. Another rule is that every time we play or do something, we have to get permission. We must buy it. We have to pay. So everybody has their pockets full of money. We put up some old metal boxes, and every time I want to make a change, I will put in a coin. I pay to be allowed. The others watch, and if they think that it's interesting, then Okay, you get money. So all the time, you hear the sound of money. In the most unlikely places there comes this horrible clinking.

This is all done to create unpredictability. I know more or less the story that I want to tell. A little girl from Colombia comes to Europe to look for her father. In a small society, slowly she discovers that her father may be an illegal immigrant worker who is missing, a drug dealer who is in hiding, or a representative of the guerrilla movement FARC. That's the story. All the knots, because people must have all the knots. But how does it become a package? There are all these things, the clinking of money, the continual singing – that create a series of associations and references for all of us while we are working. At the same time there is action-reaction from everyone. This way we build the tissue of sensual, vibrating dynamics that exists between living human beings. Which has nothing to do with the interpretation of a text. That is one way. But it varies from performance to performance. It has to, otherwise we stagnate.

The essential

What is the essential condition for a rehearsal process to work well?

That you have actors who are patient – and who go through a very long absorption of thousands and thousands of little physical nuances, which are not the interpretation of a text. Improvisations, mistakes, reactions to melodies. We improvise very, very much, and it is really important that these improvisations are fixed. To fix material from a whole hour of improvisation is a nightmare. It takes you several days. You have to repeat it, and when you repeat, you discover that the quality or the vibrating character that the improvisation had the first time, will disappear. That's how it is, always. Because you are trying to remember something that you have forgotten. It takes a very long time – weeks – before suddenly, once it has been embodied, absorbed by your organism and you don't have to think anymore, it has a completely different power.

All this takes a very long time, and a special actor who has been taught and trained to work that way. Who doesn't ask himself, 'What does it mean?' In other words, an actor who thinks with his whole body and not just with a part of the brain. I think it is one of the tragedies about the theatre of our time that it has become much too intelligent – much too conceptual, just as art as a whole has become so conceptual. But I have been lucky, and I have made sure that my actors were trained that way. I have trained my actors myself, and of course I cannot work with actors who do not have that kind of training. They cannot understand what I am searching for. However, I have worked with classical, Asian actors, because like dancers they are used to having a physical memory. They found it exciting to use their abundance of clichés in that way. Because really, what you do when you are making all these improvisations is making thousands of little reactions – and they have built thousands of clichés, many more than those we use in everyday life. Clichés are important in order to create an original language. A poet uses clichés – words – that you can read in any newspaper, not a special work of art. The physical language of the actor is similar. They are clichés. Of course, if you have five clichés you can't write *The Divine Comedy* – but if you have four to five thousand clichés you have a completely different possibility for variations and for creating new connections.

But our time is in a hurry. Not just in Europe, but in Asia too. Things must be very, very fast. Everything has to happen fast. And such a long work process is only interesting to very strange persons!

Problems

Are there one or more problems in a rehearsal process that are always impossible to solve or that you always encounter?

I have only experienced it a few times, and yet it does exist. The actors, when they start playing, the first performance, it's just as if they are learning to swim. Of course, if you can't swim then you splash around, you swallow water. It is clear to see that the person is not enjoying being in the water. Always, even though they have been through all these long rehearsals, and the smallest details have been repeated again and again, I still have a feeling that they are learning to swim for the first time. Already in the second performance you feel a different kind of security. They become amphibious humans, a kind of crocodile who can exist both on the ground and in the water. But sometimes, some actors don't become amphibious. It has happened to me, very rarely, but it has happened. And it is a problem that I cannot solve.

Sometimes I think it has to do with their earlier experiences of theatre that have formed them on an unconscious level. It's as if it's a completely different model that they are referring to or trying to realize. The other actors are those who came here as young people – the first generation – and who saw an Odin performance and said, 'I want to perform like this.' They have accepted all the curious, paradoxical work processes, because they accept that that is, presumably, how they will achieve the form of acting that we want.

The other problem… Many problems are connected with me. For example, when I can see that there is already a very good solution to something or other, and it works, and yet I am not satisfied. Imagine that your thing is 8,750 metres and I say, 'Damn it, no, it has to be 8,284 metres!' It is a nightmare for the actors, because they don't really understand what the director is after. And I don't know either. But I know that there is a difference of ten to twenty metres, or two hundred metres. I must say I am really impressed that my actors have put up with me. But it is not a problem, it is more like a sorrow inside me. Because I know that I am forcing them to do something, yet I know that if we make it together the performance will have a different… Then something else happens, not for all the spectators, but for some of them.

Dreams

If you could change anything in the work process, what would you change?

I know it's terrible, but I think I have had everything that I have wanted from life. And I have been able to realize all my wishes. What I want I can realize. There is a very practical limitation – money – but on the other hand I have always believed and still do that the people are the most important thing and not the money. That people solve every problem related to money. As long as I am capable of keeping this environment, an environment of people, we'll be alright. We all need to earn our daily bread. But it is not the most important thing. The most important thing is something else. As long as this something else exists, I think it is very, very easy to make theatre.

Interview: Barbara Simonsen

Eugenio Barba (I/DK)
Eugenio Barba (born 1936) is artistic director and founder of Odin Teatret. During the past fifty years he has directed more than seventy productions with Odin Teatret and the intercultural Theatrum Mundi Ensemble. In 1979 he founded ISTA – International School of Theatre Anthropology. His unique work method has been developed from his friend and colleague Jerzy Grotowski's physical actors' training and voice work, and together with Odin Teatret he has developed the 'barter', a way of exchanging cultural expressions with a community within the structure of a performance.

Select works
Brecht's Ashes (1980)
The Gospel According To Oxyrhincus (1985)
Mythos (1998)
The Chronic Life (2011)

Website
www.odinteatret.dk

3

Jérôme Bel

Why

Why did you choose to work in theatre?

It is a question that I'm asking myself at the moment. Because lately I have been asked to do films and exhibitions, and I was very happy about that, I thought it would interest me much more – but it hasn't caught my interest. So I think that theatre is truly a necessity for me, but I am still searching. I am wondering why it is in this particular space that something happens for me. I don't know yet. Why is it that this construction, this structure, where some people are doing something in the light while others are sitting in the dark watching, has triggered such a longing in me to engage? I don't know.

How

Can you describe your work method, from the idea to the finished product? How do you choose the theme for your next performance?

I believe that every performance needs its own individual form of production. I would have to explain them one by one, because to me the form of production determines the project. Of course, there are some general guidelines. For example, I don't like to rehearse. I rehearse as little as possible, because to me rehearsals are not theatre. Rehearsals have nothing to do with what will happen in reality. My dream would be to make a performance in one day and play it in the evening. That is sort of what I'm doing at the moment. I make performances where I'm working on stage and not in a studio during the day. As long as there are no spectators it isn't theatre.

At one time I involved an audience in the rehearsals. There were two hundred people watching the rehearsals for a week. It was interesting, because we talked to each other. In fact, they were rehearsing with me and they became part of the performance. The rehearsals determine the result, so you have to be extremely careful about this thing that you call rehearsals. Terrible word. It's alright in English, but in French: 'répétitions', it's awful. To repeat, to do it again. Not stimulating at all. So I try to avoid rehearsals as much as possible, so that the work can continue on stage and the performers will not be able to say, 'There, it's finished, we have no more rehearsals, we don't have to work anymore, we only have to play it.' That doesn't interest me at all.

I have a repertoire company, which means we perform the same shows for several years. We have to continue working, otherwise it becomes very boring and exactly that: a repetition. If you repeat, the essence of theatre vanishes, this here and now, this constant conscience of being in the present and not just repeating what one did the night before, although naturally that is also inevitable. The performers of my company, who do a good job, are preoccupied with questions like that. And I'm fascinated by them. How can I maintain a presence? How can I push this reflection philosophically? What is the difference between yesterday, the day before yesterday, and today? Even though you are in the same theatre, and you have done this show for ten years? Something will have changed, of course. There is one more day of my life, there is one more show, there is an audience that is different from yesterday and the day before. I think that's very important.

Do you have a method that prevents the performers from just repeating?

Yes. First of all, I talk with them a lot after the performances. There are always technical problems, and when I watch the performance I can see that things have changed. I understand new things myself, naturally. It becomes a kind of micro-surgery: 'In that moment your right arm has gone up a bit further that it usually does, and that fits better with the rest.' You keep elaborating and polishing. I love that.

I don't understand how they do it, those of my colleagues who don't make a lot of performances. I create many performances, and that's how I have learnt everything. Watching what has happened on stage. A microscopic change that made the audience laugh, or the opposite. So my method is to talk a lot with the performers, giving them notes, being very precise. 'Move your head a bit more like this,' and so on. I'm sure that that's what theatre is about, and dance even more so.

Does that continue after the opening as well?

Oh yes, sure. Ten years later, fifteen years later I will continue saying, 'This is not working and this is okay. That thing is new, why did you do that, but it's good…' I am their continuity. And we argue a lot, because maybe three years ago I said that something was supposed to be like this and now it has to be like that. It's like an old couple. But that is the price you pay for making theatre. And I love it.

Taking it from the beginning, do you work with a co-creative process, or a theme? Do you invite performers?

No, in the beginning when I was less well known, I had my own ideas or wishes. I always had what I call material. I would define a set of material to work with. For the first performance it was objects, everyday household objects. After that it was nudity, the naked bodies of the dancers. Then, because I had worked with nudity I wanted to work with costumes. It's a bit of a long story, but I found modern costumes more 'evolved', so to speak. So I worked with the t-shirt. Then I worked with dance quotations from other choreographers. And so on.

So I would select a material that had a certain logic in relation to my artistic problems. Now, for the last four or five years I haven't come up with any ideas, or rather, I haven't had time, because now people come up with ideas for me. Now theatre directors invite me to do something for them. So I don't have time to do the things I want; I respond to other people's ideas. Actually, they are more contexts than ideas, for example, the piece *Véronique Doisneau* [2004]. I was invited by the Paris Opera, and I asked myself what I wanted to do. I started visiting the opera and I found out that it had to be a piece *about* the opera. There is something so strange about the Paris Opera, so extraordinary and so terrible that I had to talk about the place. On the other hand when I'm invited to Thailand it is of course Thailand that I talk about [*Pichet Klunchun and myself*, 2005]. There it's not about my small Parisian problems. And the latest piece that I have done was commissioned by Pina Bausch and is about one of her dancers [*Lutz Förster*, 2009].

I realize that it's a bit of a problem for me that I'm always responding to invitations. I work in a very contextual way now. I look at the context, analyse it, ask myself what will make sense here, what has not been done before. What can I bring to this? It's good though, because I'm collaborating with people. It's lively. I used to be alone, and it was great – but now I'm always in collaboration. I never work by myself anymore. It's brilliant. My obsession is no longer with myself and my ideas, it's collaboration. At the Paris Opera as well. It was Véronique who gave me the material. It was her story and that's what we used. She said things that I didn't agree with, but she was the project, and she had the right. It was a kind of tolerance that I was astonished that I had. The same goes for *Pichet* [*Pichet Klunchun and myself*, 2005] – that almost became a love story, but there were also things that I didn't agree with. In any case, it's clearly a new period since *Véronique* and 2004. From 1994 to 2004, I was always alone, but since then it has been only collaborations.

Is one of your methods to do thorough research to avoid using old images and procedures?

Yes. For example at the Paris Opera I observed, I was very vigilant, and for two years I went to all the performances. My research is scientific, which means I like to use theoretical sources to verify my ideas – I generally use Western thinkers as my tool – to ascertain if they are relevant or not. Or I use art history to verify things. What has been done? How was it received? What did it mean when someone did this or someone painted that? Because I know that it's a similar image and I try to compare, to see what it has produced and whether it is what I want to produce or not. And to see what I can reproduce. It's the kind of work that I really enjoy, the reflections and the analyses of my ideas before I stage them.

The essential

What is essential for a rehearsal or creation process to succeed?

To me it's that it moves quickly. When it becomes long, I know that it won't work, because it means that people don't understand what I'm asking of them. As I said in the beginning, I don't like to rehearse. In general, why do we rehearse [répéter]? Because people don't understand what they are supposed to do. That's why we rehearse. And so ever since the beginning I decided to do things that are very, very simple. On purpose, in order to not have to rehearse them. It means that we spend more time thinking about what it means, why are we doing it, what is the impact on the audience, is it historically valid – rather than working and rehearsing to synchronize this or that complicated movement. To get rid of this kind of 'laborious' work was a choice made from the beginning.

As a spectator I admire when people do complicated things in dance, but I know that I would not be interested in it, and that I would soon be bored with it. So I avoid it. I ask the actors to do very simple things so that we don't have to rehearse them. Technically, my performances are also very simple. So that I don't have to spend hours in the theatre. I prefer to go to museums or read books rather than rehearse and repeat the same things over and over again.

I need a lot of time for myself in my work, however, because I think and write a lot. I can think about a performance for a year, two years… I'll think about it during breakfast, or while I'm on the tube or riding my bike. But what I am talking about is the time that I spend together with the performers. I need that to be very short, because socially I find it difficult and very tiring. So I try to reduce that time, but on the other hand I try to think out the meeting with them very, very precisely. What they are going to do, how they are going to do it. I can be very controlling.

Now, with my new project, thanks to new technology I am able to work through emails. That means we don't rehearse; they have to produce a text, and like Véronique Doisneau they have to tell the story of their life. So all we need is for them to establish this narrative. Working through emails is brilliant. It means there isn't all this 'hello – how are you', and we don't have to move around. I can read them whenever I want; when I have time I open the emails and I know that there will be a new version of the text. I have a family now and I try to travel less. So it suits me really well.

Then there is Skype. This video thing. We can also rehearse through Skype now. The dancers that I work with are also travelling all around the world, so if I am in Hong Kong I can talk to a dancer who is in Mexico – even though he is German and I am French. We can continue working together. These are methods of rehearsal that are just… I'm still astonished by them myself. I can actually rehearse through the internet. It's really a wonderful thing, both from an economic and an ecological perspective. We reduce the travelling, the costs. There is no space, which I find great. There is a kind of dissolution of space. I'm sure it changes the result. The production method will create a different performance. I love it. As soon as I discovered that these things could happen in a totally new way, I was really excited.

So to get back to your question, what is the condition for things to go well… Rapidity is one thing. In the sense that there is communication. That we're at the same speed mentally and psychically. And for things to go well – in this respect I'm extremely radical – I will cancel. I cancel the performance. The moment I feel that the rehearsals are not going well, I cancel the performance, I send everybody home, I tell them, 'Sorry, this is not going to work out.' And I do it more and more often. I know it's a bit radical. I have just cancelled a show, for example. I did it, because the dancer wasn't able to answer one of my questions. But I really believe that this part of the production process is so important that if there are already problems of communication here we are never going to solve them. And if we haven't solved a problem during the rehearsal process it is out of the question to put it on stage. If we haven't found anything... If we haven't found anything we will not show the performance. My process can be described like this: I have a problem, I put it forward, and the performance has to solve it. If I don't find a solution it is of no interest to me, and I don't think it will be to an audience either.

Is there a connection between a good rehearsal process and a good performance? The better the rehearsals, the better the result?

No. Although, I'm not sure... There is a sort of tradition that says that if things go badly the performance will go well, but obviously it's one of those foolish, superstitious traditions that theatre likes to wallow in. It's terrible. No, in general when I do a production and I go through with it to the end, these productions that I have now have all been touring for about ten years. The process can't be bad, because this community of people that come together for a performance have to feel good together. It's very hard to recover afterwards, if something bad has happened. Generally, you can't.

To return to your question, I think that if things have gone badly, it's certain that you will feel it in the performance. I think that you will see on stage what has happened during rehearsals. Even though you smile and make a nice face, if things have gone really badly it will show. I will be able to see from the performance if the rehearsals have gone well or not. And I have lots of friends in the business that I can ask afterwards, and they will say, 'Yes, yes, it's been horrible!' Even if it's a play about happiness or whatever, and it's their role to make us believe, I will see that that is not what has happened. I see the opposite. And in general, the performance will not be good.

What you are trying to make always has to carry on all levels. The actor has to be carried by the exact question that you are posing. As a spectator you will then have not only the voice represented, but also see the reality of the work and the reflections that the performer has had. With me, with… I can't prove this theory, of course, but I'm almost sure of it. What you see on stage is what has happened during rehearsals. Basically. That's why, when rehearsals are going badly, it is better to leave it.

Problems

Is there a problem that cannot be solved in rehearsals? Is there a situation, a problem, an experience that you've never been able to resolve?

Yes. As I have told you, I know a lot about what I'm looking for. Which means I never work with improvisation. But once, since the majority of people around me work with improvisation I thought, well, maybe they are right after all, maybe I should do like them – and I did it. And it went very, very badly [*laughs*]. I will never work with improvisation again. First of all, I have doubts about this kind of work. But of course, there are people who do it. It just doesn't suit me at all. It is out of the question that everyone starts off like that, doing whatever they want, expressing themselves. No. That's not my method.

To me, the problem with improvisation is that it presupposes a freedom. We improvise because we assume that we can be free. Only, from the point of view of the human and social sciences it has been proven that nobody is free. That we are totally constructed by and conformed with our own culture, by what we have seen and so on. And I noticed that a lot of the things that came out of certain performers in an 'authentic' way were actually forgotten memories of things that they had seen and liked. And I find that extremely problematic. Because what has happened is then exactly the opposite. And so it doesn't interest me at all. I start from the opposite principle. The question is for example: What is your conformism? How can you free yourself from what you have learnt, from what others want you to say? How can you find a subjectivity? Because a priori, being an artist is exactly that.

Finding a subjective voice that stands out from the general discourse. At least for a contemporary artist. Because contemporary art is trying to produce new ideas. New discourses.

What I try to do when I interview dancers – and I think it shows in the performances that I'm doing at the moment – is to say for example, 'You have produced something in the big companies (because that's who I'm working with at the moment), and what is your opinion about that? What is the reality of that? Your reality as a Thai dancer or a classical dancer at the Paris Opera.' They are famous practices in dance history; okay, identified, labelled. But you, you have served this tradition, you have been one of the performers in this big company, and what happens inside, for you? What has been the story from a subjective point of view? What I have realized is that you hear the critics, you hear the choreographer, you sometimes hear the audience, but you don't hear the dancers very much. And yet it seems to me that they form the most precise experience of dance. They are the ones who do it. Who transmit it. They are the medium between the choreographer and the audience. The choreographer is no longer there. The audience comes after. But the moment when it happens – they produce that, and that is what interests me. To let this discourse and this experience be heard.

My work is always reflective, in the sense that we go back to the experiences of the dancers. And we analyse. Whereas improvisation is to forget, but that's false. No one forgets. Conscience is this enormous thing, you don't even realize how much you produce with it. But sure, improvisation has served for example Steve Paxton[1] well at a certain time, it was a method for him, and it could have disappeared after that. Just as pointe shoes should have just served the makers of Giselle or whoever it was who added that; it was a really good idea, a costume idea, in fact. After that they should have disappeared. There are inventions like that that are useful then and there. I just think you should invent your own thing every time, although I know of course that we are not without history, and that I also use procedures that come from others. Maybe it was a bit stupid what I just said!

Dreams

What would you want to change or try out in a rehearsal process, if anything was possible? No limits, physical, biological or ethical.

As I've just said, I think I do the opposite of that. I certainly don't have any utopias – I don't like the word. It's an illusion in itself. On the contrary, I work within limits. What interests me is to see the limits, to mark them, and then to reach them and see if I can push them. Increase the circle, the territory of dance. I try to enlarge this territory. And exactly for this reason I think that I would be very bad without limits.

That is why the contexts – like for example the Paris Opera, I can't do everything there, certainly not the same things that I do in my own company, like doing naked performances or pissing on stage, or doing nothing. When I am at the Paris Opera I know that I am in a context that is extremely defined. And I start to ask myself, what are the limitations of the Paris Opera? What is the outline of the territory? What is acceptable? How is it defined? And when I have that – the two years of watching all the performances, studying the repertoire, the works, the dancers, the newspaper articles – I suddenly realize more or less precisely where there is a weak point. And how can I pull that out? It has to be a point that means something to me, that I want to pull out. One that is hiding, for example, it's hiding its face, it's not talked about. I look for what is hidden. There are reasons for hiding, often political ones. And so I pull this out, and it grows, suddenly there is a whole forest appearing. For the audience it's good, because that's what we are looking for. Something new. Something that we feel, but which hasn't been said.

But the dream could also be to have extreme limits – or to work with a certain person?

Yes, but I don't really know. I don't dream. Is there a desire – because that's really what the question is… These last few years, as I have said, I've been really busy. It just goes on and on, the responses to people. Before, I was all alone, and nobody helped me, nobody wanted me for years, and there was a kind of purity to that. I worked for art's sake. I didn't work for me or for my reputation or anything like that. I didn't care. What my desire produced was to make performances that were important. And to return to your first question – why theatre – I think that as a spectator I have had the strongest emotional experiences of my life. When I was sitting in a theatre seat. And I think that's what I wanted to reproduce. It's different now, as I've told you. But the desire was that. To be able – or to hope to be able – to create experiences that were as intense as those that I had received. And it was also to give them back to those who had created them for me. Now I work with Pina Bausch's dancers or Merce Cunningham's, and I'm doing a piece with Anne Teresa de Keersmaeker. These people who were the shock for me. By the most incredible luck I had started dancing and I saw these three choreographers. I was eighteen, I didn't know anything, and I saw those three. The three greatest choreographers in the last half of the twentieth century. And it was such a shock, emotionally, aesthetically, intellectually, that I think my goal was to try to give that back.

Yes, maybe that was it. I don't know. In any case, this is where all your questions today have led me to. I found it [*laughs*]. Eureka!

Interview: Isabelle Reynaud

Jérôme Bel (FR)
Jérôme Bel (born 1964) started choreographing in 1994 and has become one of the leading figures in the movement of non-dance. He provokes and entertains audiences with concepts that challenge the conventions of performance. Bel's performances have toured all over the world.

Select works
Shirtologie (1997)
The Show Must Go On (2001)
Véronique Doisneau (2004)
Gala (2015)

Website
www.jeromebel.fr

Note

1 Steve Paxton, born 1939, American dancer and choreographer, developer of the dance form contact improvisation.

4

Rachel Chavkin

Why

Why did you choose theatre, or how did you end up in theatre?

I grew up getting taken to see theatre a lot as a kid. I grew up in the D.C. area, and both my folks are civil rights lawyers and pretty political. And I very much grew up with a sense that theatre is a strong agent of social change and that culture is a huge part of where our thinking about things get shaped. So we would see everything from really terrible dinner theatre musicals to touring productions to, I guess a little bit of more – I don't know if you want to say edgier arts stuff, growing up. But I was also playing soccer and very much an athlete and not necessarily so focused on doing theatre as a kid. End of high school I decided that I did want to pursue theatre and study it, so I came to NYU [New York University], and it was here that I began seeing The Wooster Group, Elevator Repair Service, Theatre de Complicite when they were here with the show *Mnemonic*, William Forsythe's work at BAM [Brooklyn Academy of Music]. I just began seeing everything and in part because the tickets were cheaper I saw a huge amount of stuff in the downtown and more experimental scene, and found that that was absolutely where I was drawn to. So that definitely further shaped the type of theatre that I wanted to do – but yeah, I just quite loved it.

What happened in high school to make you go in that direction?

I was definitely one of those kids who did a lot of activities. And I ended up going to a summer theatre camp. I went there for six, seven years and I just really, more than anything, liked the community. Like a lot of summer camps that was where I ended up finding my drive.

In my recollection it was quite sudden that I thought, I want to do this professionally, or I want to try to continue with this. I was acting, and I acted all through college, but I also did begin directing in high school. I did an incredibly poor production of a short Christopher Durang play that I didn't really get any of the jokes in, now in retrospect [*laughs*], but I chose the NYU and specifically the programme at Playwrights Horizons Theater School at NYU, because I could both direct and act. So even then I knew that I was interested in directing. And then I took a class at NYU called COW – Creating Original Work – which was actually not even a formal class when I took it, it was this like underground class taught Sunday nights from 7 to 10 pm in a studio that was vacant, by this incredible woman Marleen Pennison who came out of the dance world, had been an experimental dancer, and was thrilling and probably the best teacher I ever had. The only assignment for that class was to be interesting alone on stage for ten minutes. And so through the course of the semester you didn't get graded, you didn't… You were the governor of how the semester shaped. And either you just didn't bring in anything all through the semester and when it got to the final showing you made up something, or people would bring in and toss out stuff every week. And through the process of that you basically learned how to set up a process. For me I learned that I needed assignments, I needed prompts. And so I began making prompts for myself.

How

That is basically how The TEAM still works today. I will give prompts and assignments to the company to generate material in response to whatever the ideas are, or images, research are that we're talking about. It might be that we need to learn about a specific thing. The show that The TEAM is going to be premiering this summer at the Edinburgh International Festival started with its roots in the Scottish Enlightenment and so one of the very first prompts was, everyone pick a philosopher from the Scottish Enlightenment, or an accompanying figure – because I actually ended up doing Walter Scott, a novelist who was deeply regressive and making work in reaction to the kind of revolution that was coming out of the Enlightenment. So the first assignment was just basically to present a book report on one of these figures [*laughs*]. Later that might evolve into: 'Okay, everyone write a scene in which x happens or these two characters meet.' And sometimes it might be doing a long-form improv between these two characters. There is no specific shape, it's always just about identifying what the problem or challenge is in a given moment, which could be: 'We need characters.' And then structuring an assignment that will address that challenge.

Can you describe a typical rehearsal process for you, as concretely as possible?

There is definitely no comparison between a rehearsal process for The TEAM and a rehearsal process for my freelance work. Actually, even the words rehearsal process are probably misnomers with The TEAM, because to me rehearsal implies working on and refining an agreed upon set of things that are going to happen. Which could be – the dialogue, that's going to get spoken, or the staging, storytelling. I've just directed a show last year called *Small Mouth Sounds* [Ars Nova, 2015] by a writer named Beth Wohl, and that was set on a silent meditation retreat, so there was almost no spoken dialogue, but a huge amount of structured physical events that would happen. Rehearsal, as I think about it, is deciding how those events are going to be. Whereas with The TEAM we can't rehearse until we've made the thing, so actually for a TEAM process which might be anywhere from a year and a half to, typically closer to three to five years, even, most of that process is 'what the hell are we doing?' Literally, what are we making, what's going to happen, why are we doing it, who are the people? So The TEAM tends to start with an overall investigation. Probably the clearest example that I can give is with *Mission Drift* [2011], we started with me asking the company to think about the question: What defines American capitalism specifically versus capitalism as it has taken shape anywhere else in the world? And very often, because I tend to find the intellectual quite moving, but many of my company members don't, they are much more 'gutterally' [*sic*] led, and that's actually a very important friction with The TEAM, how a performer thinks versus how a director or dramaturg thinks. So I give this question, and then they roll their eyes back in their head and hate me, and then the work actually begins as they figure out where their emotional stake is. We spent a huge time for that show doing research, interviewing people… We began that work before the financial crisis happened, but then once that happened the work took on a very different spin.

Some of the early research that we did included talking to friends on Wall Street, just trying to wrap our heads around what happened, plus reading a huge number of books and articles that were coming out trying to analyse what had happened in the housing collapse. I also read this book, actually on recommendation from Linda Chapman, who is the Associate Artistic Director here [New York Theatre Workshop], called *The Island at the Center of the World* by an academic named Russell Shorto, and it was making the case that the values of capitalism and multiculturalism that we might identify as particularly American are in fact rooted not in our British ancestry, but the Dutch ancestry and specifically the colony of New Amsterdam that eventually became New York. Chapter two of that book, I think, opens with the manifest document with some of the names of the people who were on the very first Dutch settlers' boat, and there were two names, Catalina Trico and Joris Rapalje, and I was like, 'Ooh, those are our characters.' So I took them and for a long time two actors in the company were playing those characters, doing it in full period garb. And we didn't know how to tell that story and it was really awful and everyone hated it, and we ended up killing those characters for about a year of the process. Then I was thinking about them and I just flipped a switch in my brain: What if they weren't in period costumes, what if Catalina looked like Juliette Lewis from *Natural Born Killers* with the blond wig and that sort of savageness? That ended up opening the whole world for us of how to actually deal with these historically rooted figures in a totally irreverent way that could tap into this blood-pumping energy that everyone was describing Wall Street with. And what Libby [King] and ultimately Bryan [Hastert], who were the two performers who ended up playing those characters, were really turned on by was that sense of rapacious hunger. Vision, but also brutality. So that ended up being a huge key.

When you're in that research phase, everybody is researching?

Everyone's researching, because everyone's a writer with The TEAM. And it's a truly horizontal writing process, as much as I am the artistic director and so certainly shaping the day-to-day doings. A day in a rehearsal process might involve a couple of hours of character-based improv and then maybe us all sitting around the table like a television writers' room, might involve someone researching something, might involve us watching a movie or looking at a series of YouTube videos for inspiration. It can be quite open, again back to whatever we feel the piece is lacking on a given day. And that's my job, typically, to identify that lack although, of course, non-stop performers will say this sucks and this is why it sucks. But on the writing level my authorial voice does not take precedence over anyone else's authorial voice. We try to work in a series of ways, because some people are much better at typing and going into that writing mode, and some people in the company are just extraordinary at getting up on stage in character and improvising from there. *RoosevElvis* [2013], this show that we made with Libby [King] and Kristen [Sieh], was made almost entirely from improvisation.

Do you record it?

You know what, we used to record it and we found that no one would go through the video. I would occasionally, to get something, but it was just a huge waste of hard drive space. So we now do audio recording sometimes, but most of the time actually, the way we use rehearsal assistants is for transcribing as it happens. So we end up with these of course fragmentary transcripts, because my company can speak quite fast when they're getting going, but those transcripts then serve as the bones for a given project, for a given script.

Research begins to bleed into generating material. And it's the generative phase that The TEAM spends most of its time in. Of course we're continuing to research through the generative phase, there is not a day where we're like, 'Okay, now we're ready to start making.' We start making material ridiculously prematurely just to begin getting through the obvious stuff. Sometimes an image… I remember Libby very early on in the *Mission Drift* process began playing with this idea of bowling, and it was not attached to anything besides the fact that we'd had a friend in a class that we were teaching mention this television show called *Bowling for Dollars*. I think it was a local cable access show and it was just people … bowling for dollars, as you might imagine! That ends up sticking and becoming actually the physical language used for these implosions of buildings in Las Vegas, because that piece ended up being set in Las Vegas. And that bowling image ended up being what Catalina and Joris would do while you were hearing these huge crashes of buildings coming down of old Las Vegas. So you sort of never know what's going to stick around until opening night, basically. Because as I said, Catalina and Joris – when I tell people that there was a whole year of the *Mission Drift* process where those characters didn't exist they are like, 'What were you doing?' because I mean, they are the main characters, the whole play is telling their story.

So we generate huge amounts of material, and it's nothing for The TEAM to be able to generate five hundred pages of play in a week. That said, those don't all go together and more importantly they are not necessarily the show that we have any intention of making. Throughout The TEAM's process we will do workshop showings and those more than anything force us to make decisions. We try never to present a workshop that is longer than ninety minutes, because that's hard to sit through if it's unformed, and of course it's going to be unformed at that stage. We do these series of workshop showings and we may do up to five of them for a given process and get feedback from the audience, and I tend to be pretty fascist about the type of feedback that

I am willing to accept. Particularly early on. We're so not interested in whether something is clear early on, we know how to – well, we've gotten better at this as we've gotten older – we know how to tell a story arc … 'ish'! [*Laughs.*] So at least at that stage it's not a question of, are you following the characters' through line, it's about what ideas feel loaded, what images really seared onto your eyeballs? It's very sensory in the early stages. Then later, as we begin to really refine… I just left Southwest Virginia for a residency at Virginia Tech, and we're very far along into the process for this new show that we're making for the National Theatre of Scotland. There we were able to do a full reading of the script and actually were able to ask questions about character arc and what information did you feel you were missing about a character. Also what images in the text – this was a reading so it was less physical than sometimes our other workshops might be – are searing your brain?

And is that the last phase?

So *then* – and it took us many years to get to this – what we realized was that it was incredibly helpful if we rehearsed. [*Laughs.*] Which was so stupid. But I think actually as we have all matured, we all began having processes outside The TEAM, and we realized there was this whole moment of refining and deepening and owning. Of course, The TEAM as an entity, we pathologically rewrite things and revise things in a way that no freelance writer I ever worked with, does. To profound degrees, moving entire characters, shifting whole story lines. But we now do try to carve a period that we say, this is rehearsal, and it's about activating that part of your brain as much as the writer part of your brain. And actually, discovering this over the past few years has been really profound for The TEAM's process, because we realized there were many problems that are actor or directorial problems that we were trying to solve as writers. And so you can end up with a text that is doing more work to be clear than actually would be interesting or that even any of us individually as artists would respond to. Because most of us in The TEAM tend to be moved by the more poetic, the more jagged, the more mysterious works of art. That give space for a lot. We were filling in all these gaps as writers that if you as a performer just take this moment and have all this backstory that we've made up, but we don't say it, you just live it, you don't need that paragraph necessarily. Or you need that one line. That's still a slippery part of our process, because it can be deeply hard to know on a given day whose problem it is. Whether the staging is just screwed and needs actually to be quite still, or it needs to be chaos.

So that last phase is actually starting to involve more cutting of text?

Yes, well, we cut throughout, we are constantly cutting text. Although much more surgically.

The essential

What is in your experience the essential condition for a rehearsal process to be successful or fruitful?

It really helps if there is some sort of natural light in the room. Because otherwise we go mad. That said, we have had useful, delusional rehearsals in a basement. Our rehearsal room for years was windowless. Subbasement.

I mean, us all being together is the core answer. That we have been able to afford to get everyone together. That we have enough interns or assistants to transcribe. That on a given day people are in a good mood versus a bad mood. And that either we are early enough in the process that people are still going, 'How do I find my way in this?' or we're late enough in the process that people have found what's moving them and making them fight for material, fight for a given theme. Because if people aren't passionate about getting into it in that way then the work is just brutal.

Our sound designer is often in the room; that helps. We try to always rehearse with Matt [Hubbs] in the room, basically like another performer. That's a critical health thing in the rehearsal room. Those are the main elements.

When you think of the rehearsal processes in general that you've been through, would you say there's even an essential condition for all of them?

Not beyond the people, I guess. You need good people in the room. It goes back to this thing in someone who wants to be there and is drawn to figuring stuff out. For The TEAM that's on a writing perspective, for my freelance work that could just be a performer who is trying to figure out how to inhabit or tell this story from the inside. And is willing to play, and by play I mean make up blocking, try different voices, try different intentions and ways of saying lines. They are really basic things, but to be as practical as possible, that's what I mean. And it's thrilling to work with performers who are thinking about what the overall art is that this piece is trying to get at, what the culture is that is being created, and how they might sit within that or help further that along.

Problems

What in your experience is the biggest problem or obstacle that comes up? That you can't avoid or can't solve?

It's the same answer: it's the people. On two levels, the first and foremost with The TEAM, as boring as it is, our biggest obstacle is people's schedules, which very, very rarely align. We might end up with a year when literally we can get every single member of the company into the room for a week. And then inevitably someone ends up having a conflict that week. That's part of why we have begun out of necessity making smaller shows, because all of our early work used to involve the entire company. Which was also big and expensive to tour. And of course money equals time, in America anyway, and money is hard to raise in America and New York. So I spend a huge amount of my life fundraising. I just got an email this morning about the benefit that is now a month away and we need to get invites out and blah blah blah… Another obstacle is, particularly with The TEAM, this doesn't come up in my freelance life really, because the freelance process is so much shorter and more contained, not asking of its artists in the way that The TEAM does. In The TEAM world, if someone is bracing against the project or held up against how something is going that has to get addressed, because we're a family, we've been working together for eleven years and some of us have known each other since we were seventeen. You can't brush off or proceed until that thing gets addressed. In the way that in a freelance room it's work, you are there to work and so you put forward that aura even if things are crazy inside. Maybe I'll have a performer who is having a hard time and we'll touch base about it, but it's a very different thing than what can happen in a TEAM room if something is not going well.

Dreams

If you could change or try out anything in the rehearsal process, what would you do?

For this new show with the National Theatre of Scotland we're adding music quite late to the show. It will be live music, and having musicians who are right there beside you trying to wrestle with how the story gets told is… I love it. And I spend most of my freelance directing life working with new music theatre, so that culture is very familiar to me, but not necessarily in a TEAM room. And it's a very different thing again than a freelance room where it's sort of agreed upon that, 'This is your part and this is our part, and we'll meet at the places where I have italicized the lines, those are lyrics' – to say that anything could become a lyric, or anything could get spoken. It's just one more piece of mess. How chaotic can we make it?

Interview: Barbara Simonsen

Rachel Chavkin (US)

Rachel Chavkin (born 1980) is a director, dramaturg and writer. She is the founding artistic director of the New York-based theatre company The TEAM. Since 2004, Chavkin has directed and co-authored all of The TEAM performances, and as an independent director she collaborates with writers of new work. The TEAM's performances are created through research and devising and are critical examinations of American culture and politics.

Select works

Mission Drift (2011)
RoosevElvis (2013)
Small Mouth Sounds (2015)
Natasha, Pierre & The Great Comet of 1812 (2012, 2016)

Website

www.theteamplays.org

5

Kirsten Dehlholm

Why

Why did you choose to make theatre?

I've worked with materials always, ever since I was a child. Working with giving form to materials, with structure and the sensual. And at some point in my artistic development I went from the wall, from wall objects, into the space to do three-dimensional things in surroundings. Then it became costumes, and in that way the person, the figure, the human being was brought into this 'environment' – and I just became very interested in how space, the human being and material merge together, or play with or against each other. I began by seeing some photographs by the Polish artist Tadeusz Kantor, where an orchestra playing a classical concert is placed in the sea[1], and this image really triggered something in me. Because this moving of a well-known situation into an almost absurd place really opened my eyes to the fact that if you place familiar things in a new context it makes you see both the familiar and the new in new ways.

And then I'm just very greedy for images. The language of images is my universe. And it wasn't enough for me just to have the still images, I wanted to make moving images. Slow-moving images with figures in a space. That's how I started. During the first nine years I worked without words, without text, only with space and sounds, music or movement. No special light either, really, since we often worked at museums in daylight. But later it came; when I had worked nine years without words in the Theatre of Images [Billedstofteatret 1977–85] I founded my new company Hotel Pro Forma, and there we started working with words. Since then all my performances have been an investigation of text and image, how text and image can enrich each other without becoming an illustration of each other and thereby killing each other, so to speak. I work with a universe where one and one makes three and not two.

How

First, let me say that I think it's a really good initiative, you have taken here. It's very interesting to look at the whole complex in connection with performing arts. It's interesting to focus on everything that lies behind that one hour or the few hours during which we watch a show. When you think of the endless number of hours, weeks, months and years that go into creating a performance, as audience you are in fact literally only seeing the tip of the iceberg. When the performance is over, the actors step forward and receive the audience's applause or the opposite. But the work is always a result of the effort of many people, their time, talent, experience, fight, will, and their creativity. People always ask what the performance is about. And we could of course answer that it's about this or that, the specific theme or whatever it is. But we could also answer that the performance is about logistics, about practical, and pragmatic and technical solutions to complicated problems. One could also just say that performing arts are about creating magic, about creating those rare moments outside time and space, where everything comes together or where everything is displaced through big or small explosions only to settle down again in new places and maybe with new discoveries. Maybe it's just a light-bulb moment. And that's okay too. As performing artists we want to affect the spectator; the spectator wants to be affected, to be touched, not groped – and certainly to be entertained.

Through my long life in performing arts I have tried so many different processes. Luckily, most of them have been happy. The problems have been elsewhere; they have been more about the dissemination of our works. I'll get back to that later. We start with a space, a theme, a design or something that fascinates us. And this something is always a part of the world. We call our performances investigations of the world. The performance is this investigation. The performance is a journey into the world. We do a lot of research that also brings us out into the world. So sometimes it is a real, concrete journey that we start.

Can you describe a typical process from idea to performance? Do you have specific, recurring steps or phases?

A work process consists of a lot of phases. Some of them are parallel, and some of them follow right after one another. As inspiration I might see a space that I want to make something for, because it has a very specific character. Or it might be a theme that I will look for a fitting space for. The space and the theme are always connected somehow. Then I start doing research, which can be a lot of reading, maybe travelling. But it's very important that very early on there is a concept for what kind of performance it is. Is it large or small, where is the audience placed – are they on a balcony looking vertically down at the floor from a bird's-eye view, are they facing the stage like in the Italian theatre, are they sitting on two sides or three, or is there no stage at all so they are walking around like at an exhibition? I've done performances with all these different forms. Form, content, expression, are always completely linked.

It's the same with collaboration partners. When I have a concept, the overall idea, I need to choose one, two, maybe three other artists to collaborate in developing the idea. And also the performers are chosen specifically for that project, whether they are actors, singers, dancers or other persons, typecasts. It all depends on the project at hand.

How do you work with the performers in the rehearsal process?

Again, the rehearsal processes varies very much from one project to the other, because the performances are so different and have many different conditions and circumstances. But usually we have fixed a lot of things before we go into the rehearsal space with the performers. We have made the blocking, a sort of choreography, where they are standing, what they are doing. Often also in what direction they are looking. This blocking is written down – sometimes it almost looks like musical notations. With this blocking on paper we go into the rehearsal space. Sometimes, even before we have had the performers come in, we might have had extras to make these tableaus and scenes, and then we light them. When the performers arrive, everything on stage is finished, including the lights, and they fill out the rest. That's one way of doing it, but it doesn't always happen like this. It depends who we are working with. We might also have a workshop with actors who are given various tasks, they make something, we watch and video film it. After a couple of months we meet again, and then we have made material for them. But it's very definite on our part where we want to go. We don't improvise. That's not our thing at all. It's also important that the performance must be pretty much finished well before the opening. If it's not spot on at the opening, then I have a problem. Because I actually never solve it after that.

The essential

What is essential for a good rehearsal process?

The most essential conditions are: Time, trust, good spatial conditions and a reasonable economy. Starting with the economy, of course it's a basic condition no matter whether you have a small or a large amount of money. You have to know what you're dealing with. Naturally, we always apply for more money, that's normal for a cultural institution or anywhere, because the ambitions are always threatening to blow the budget. It's not because more money automatically makes a better performance. Sometimes on the contrary. The most important thing is that we work according to the means available. And we always have to be super-creative, and innovative, and ingenious to make a lot out of a little. But that's not a bad thing. It's a challenge. Having a framework is always good, having a wall to play against, and we do. But a place where we often feel the lack of means is in the number of employees, especially in public relations. It takes a lot of money to make a good dissemination, and we are always short. That's a bit of a needle's eye. Because there are many cultural offers out there, and we need to be seen.

About the spatial conditions: it means a lot that we have good spaces and facilities for our rehearsal process, and good, exciting spaces in which to show our performances. We also like to have enough time to explore the possibilities that the spaces give us. That can be hard to get at the specific places where we go.

Then there is trust. We are working with a lot of unknown factors in the artistic and collaborative process. Here it's important that we believe in the people we have chosen to be a part of the artistic development process. We need to be able to trust that they can develop their part of the performance, and they are given a responsibility. There are all the employees, and there are all the other collaboration partners, for example co-producers. Here it's about trust as well, but mainly about economy. It's a tough fight all the way. No soft values. Both they and we need to get something out of it.

Time is a very important factor in our work processes. It takes one to three years to develop a performance, because we always start from scratch. We have been working like that for many years. It takes time to get through the many layers of complexity that the performance consists of. That's how it has to be. Making images takes time. Experiencing images takes time. By seeing the performance once the spectator might only experience the topmost layer, and some will experience more layers. If you come several times you will experience even more layers. But that's not important. The performance must be made so that you can experience it on many levels. It has been possible for us to work with these long processes because for many years we have been fortunate enough to be supported by the Danish Arts Council. Even though every year or every second year we have to apply for this support, that is never given automatically. We still have to prove that we are good enough, even after thirty years.

Every performance is essentially different from the others. That means every time new processes, new collaboration partners, new conditions, new constellations. And as we know, everything changes with the context. The context is probably the only stable thing in the entire process. We use the context as a framework and as a wall to play against, as a starting point for the performance.

Every new performing arts work is the result of a collaboration between a lot of people. Professional artists from all genres, scientists. It is probably one of the greatest lessons in my experience during all these years that I have always worked together with other people, and as a result of that, the work always becomes bigger than yourself. It's a joy to be part of these processes, and I come out of them with more knowledge and more consciousness about myself and about the world. And with new surprises, because I want to be surprised. I want to let things happen, I want to know, I want to make others take me to new places where I haven't been before.

It is also an important experience that it's essential to change between performance sites, between large and small formats. Each work is created for buildings of interesting architecture or for different kinds of stages. Through the use many different kinds of places to perform, everything changes: form, and content, and expression. That these are linked is also an important realization. That the design is a very big part of the content, that it's part of the narrative, and that sometimes it *is* the narrative. We work with perception so that our performances will be perceived first through the senses and then afterwards speak to the brain. When that succeeds it is a performance that you won't forget.

I've realized that the architectural, the physical surroundings, always play an important part. Both the architecture in itself and the function of the place, whether it's a museum, a theatre, a city hall, a school, a swimming bath or whatever it may be. The place is always a co-performer in the show, and very often it's our starting point. We will often do performances that are created directly for the dimensions of the architecture and related to the function of the place. It's important and interesting to bring performing arts works to places where you don't normally present them, because it gives you a different audience. We avoid the expectations that people often have of a theatre performance in a theatre space. But it's just as important to reverse the character of the works that are shown in different places. For example to show more experimenting works on the big stages of the theatre and the opera, just as you could show more classical works on smaller, alternative stages. Performing arts in general; we and the audience move around in ghettos and in very fixed categories, really. We go to the same places, and therefore it would be enriching if we could open up and expand the borders of what is being shown and done in certain places. This dialogue between functions, traditions, art and culture is always important. It's a very long process to change our habits, and it's a never-ending one.

Problems

Have you experienced recurring problems in your process?

I suppose the problem is, really, that the subjects I choose are always very big. They are always much bigger than ourselves. It may be money, it may be China, the double, twins, genetic engineering. Education or Darwin. Well, is it a problem? I don't know, but I certainly take on very big subjects. In the performance *jesus_c_odd_size* in 2000 and 2002 it was Jesus and Christianity. So there is always a lot of research to do and therefore also a lot of choices to make. How do we want to present this? We don't narrate in naturalism or in plots or action. We narrate through statements and images, music, atmosphere, and we always invent a set of rules for each production. You have to follow a certain colour code or certain materials, or the performers have to do things in a very specific way. Rules that are changed with each production.

Insoluble problems are for example that we never know where it ends, that we never know what the result is actually going to be, or how it will be received. Those are the conditions. As soon as we start focusing on that it becomes about doing something commercial

– which is fine, but it's a totally different market, and it's not at all where we create art. That doesn't mean, however, that we don't think about what it's all about or how people should experience it or understand it. It just doesn't come first. It's not where we start.

Dreams

Is there something you dream of trying, if everything was permitted and possible?

Now, this is actually the hardest question. Yes, what if? My first 'what if' priority is not so much about having better rehearsal facilities, more money for production, or being able to use the best actors and singers. It's about the dissemination of our works. It's about being allowed to show our performances in far corners of the world, where people are not used to seeing this kind of art.

The dissemination of our performances has poor conditions. The performances are much too expensive because of the high salaries that we pay in this country compared to other countries. Expenses for transport are of course also very high. It's a big world, but not for the performing arts of the Western world. Here we move in very small circles in very certain countries with certain festivals. My dream is to go to other countries, like Eastern Europe, the Middle East, Asia, South America, or to go to Greenland or China or far into Russia. And not with one of the small, light performances, with one of the big performances shown full-scale. So that these countries wouldn't be fobbed off with something small. It would also be very interesting and exciting to create works in these same countries with local performers and use their talents and traditions in a new context.

Another wish would be to create a work for the great entrance hall of the Tate Modern in London, for example. Or other wonderful architectural houses and buildings around the world. It would also be interesting to use a modern stage with all its technical facilities and let the stage technics be the protagonist. Making performances, open works, where you keep the text as well as the images in a state of the unfinished. For example letting the large sets that are coming in, or out, or up, or down, stay hanging there before they fall into place. Thereby seeing what is coming and not yet finished. And then you have to think for yourself; as audience, you have to finish it yourself. That would take an incredible amount of stage time, though. And stage time on one of the big, modern stages I suppose is the nearest we can get to utopia today.

It annoys me that experimenting theatre is usually referred to the small stages in the big houses. That you are not using the big stage to set the whole machinery in motion for the experiment. It's very rare. We have tried, though, to make large productions of an experimental nature that can *only* be shown at a big stage, and we have succeeded in touring with them, but only in Western Europe. Right now we are working on a new kind of opera [*Tomorrow in a Year*, 2009] that will be shown at the big venues, still only in Western Europe. If only we could show a performance like that in Mali or Vietnam or Greenland.

Any other dreams or wishes?

I haven't worked with actors very much. It hasn't been my primary interest, because traditionally actors have a totally different education and focus than what I have had. But I think it would be a challenge to work with actors and also with psychological texts. I have tried it, but only on a small scale. And I do think it's very, very interesting to challenge the psychological texts and the psychological theatre with my form of theatre, with my stage designs and blockings where the space still plays a very important role in the narrative and in relation to the text. I would like to explore that further.

With classically trained actors?

Yes. Classically trained actors do have something, absolutely. I just think that the performance as a whole is often too digested and over-interpreted for me as a spectator. It has all become a gravy. So there is nothing for me to chew. As a spectator I always want there to be something I don't understand. I have to be on the edge of my seat as a spectator. And so I'm not interested in seeing the actor coming all the way up to me with his or her interpretation and presentation of the psychological aspect. I think it's super-exciting to work with the entire psychological universe, but doing it in a theatrically interesting framework so that the text might even stand out more clearly, because it's not being interpreted, just said. So we might really *hear* the words. I've done Ibsen like that, and we really *heard* the words, and they had a very strong meaning, because they weren't played or overplayed.

Interview: Deborah Vlaeymans

Kirsten Dehlholm (DK)
Kirsten Dehlholm (born 1945) founded her performance theatre company Hotel Pro Forma in 1985. Originally a visual artist, she takes her starting point in a space or a theme through which she investigates the world. She often chooses as performers people who have certain characteristics or skills, and she regularly includes objects and actions that are not normally associated with performing arts. Her performances have toured extensively all over the world.

Select works
Operation: Orfeo (1993)
I Only Appear to be Dead (2005)
War Sum Up (2011)
Cosmos+ (2014)

Website
www.hotelproforma.dk

Note

1 Tadeusz Kantor, *The Panoramic Sea Happening* (1967).

6

Maxine Doyle

Why

Why did you choose to work with theatre and dance?

I had an amazing teacher at my secondary school who ran a dance club. She was very passionate and really inspired my love affair with contemporary dance. I am obsessed with dancing and the magic of theatre because of this very special woman.

How

How do you go from idea to performance? How does it all start?

I will try to talk mainly about Punchdrunk, but with a focus on my own approach. My approach… Well, it's difficult to talk singularly about it, because it's really collaborative, with a big creative team and everything feeds in. But essentially, we're always looking for a building. We haven't really conceived yet a show where it isn't about the building, or about space, or about site. Members of the team – especially Felix [Barrett], that's his drive – are very excited about the experience of site and the building, whereas I tend to use the text as a starting point. I start to daydream about the text and how I imagine that world: that world appearing and revealing itself. So in my process I start with the text. I start with the score or the sources, whether that might be the music sources that we're interested in, or film sources, art works. And then I look through to try to identify particular kinds of ideas. For me it's a process of stripping down to something that is very easy. Easily digestible and manageable or translatable. I just strip the text down to try and find individual ideas and then look at the kind of company that we're going to be working with on that project in terms of performers.

For both Felix and me, the performers are really, really important. We have a core company, not a regular company, but a group of people that we have worked with regularly over the last five years, and they offer a combination of particular skills – physical skill, choreographic skill – and a kind of presence that is very enigmatic and charismatic. As an audience member, you can be really drawn to them. So I suppose that I start to invent, and the creative process begins when I start to dream about the ideas and these people. And the ideas start to become alive when I start to imagine how a performer might embody these ideas. Casting the show is for us a huge part of the process.

We cast a combination of performers we work with regularly that we really trust, and then particularly we try to identify new artists who might be filling a gap or a hole. And for me I suppose the most exciting part of the process happens in the rehearsal studio, as opposed to on site. Even though we are a site-based company and the work is driven by the building, it is really important that we have this protected time off site, which might be two, three or four weeks. And actually, I suppose in my dreams I would always have longer off site and longer on-site time. The off-site time is really protected, because that is essentially where the writing happens. When I say writing, I mean the writing of the body, the physical language or the visual language.

How do you start working with the performers in the rehearsal studio?

Everybody comes to the rehearsal studio equipped with a sense of context and a kind of knowledge of the starting points of the sources. But we're not an acting company, so it's a different… It's interesting; people come with impressions rather than a deep psychological understanding of the work. People have their impressions; they have their senses. I always start with lots of music. It's not necessarily music that ends up in the work. It's music to use as a stimulus, as a catalyst to provoke responses and to provoke reactions. My main process is improvisation, so we spend a long time in the beginning of every day – I mean at least a good hour and a half even to two hours – doing a warm-up, which leads into extensive improvisations. It feels really important for my work to set up a very safe, nurturing environment for all of us to work together in. I'm not a director that thrives on tension or fear or aggression. Our work has to be really collaborative, so I really need to feel that I can be open with all of the performers, and that I get that back from them. Because ultimately in our work we are asking people to give a lot, we are asking people to trust, to go to places of emotional danger, places of emotional depth, and to really expose themselves and to put themselves out there as people as well as performers. It's important that the place in which we work is really supportive. One of the ways that we do that is through this concentrated focus of the warm-up process, which happens in the morning. And it shifts, but in general we tend to work with the principles of contact improvisation as a way into moving. I'm drawn to contact, because in its ethos and its origins it's about inclusion, it's about support, it's about expressions. It feels important that people have a real sense and opportunity to play for themselves in the beginning of a workday, without a particular agenda to create and to make.

Often what happens is that we start with these long warm-ups, and then I work very instinctively. It's about being very present in the moment and seeing what is unfolding before me, and shifting it and shaping and throwing… We might set up an improvisation, and what I don't like doing is stopping and talking, and stopping and talking. So we don't sit down very much, we don't sit around a table. People might play for an hour or two hours, and I keep throwing things into the studio to shift it, whether it is changing the music, or bringing in props or shifting with an object, setting up games, setting up structures. It feels like the process is really organic and it's really immediate. And it feels a little bit like pottery, it's like you are crafting these events moment to moment as they are emerging.

Often we film a lot of the improvisations and then for me it's a process of taking that away with me and scrolling through the improv, looking and pulling for moments and situations. Sometimes that's very literal; we lift language and the dancers recreate that, or a theme emerges and we go back and replay that theme or idea. Or a texture comes up, or a tone. It's about looking for little signals and symbols, a little science to navigate the way through to create the language. The studio is a safe space physically, so I am always very happy when we get a really good studio to work in. Sometimes we don't manage it and we work in less exciting rehearsal studios, but it makes a massive difference to my process if we are in a space that's clean, and warm, and big, where you can have coffee, where you can rest, where you can focus. I think it makes a huge difference. We did a research period in Florida last year or the year before, at White Oak with The Sundance [Institute Theatre Lab], investigating a project that hopefully we'll be doing next year. And it's a beautiful nature retreat, and the studio is in the middle of nature and the food is amazing, the studio is amazing, there's loads of support, and it just really opens you up to lots of possibilities. So the studio time is really protected.

So in the beginning it's about play, it's about navigation, it's about sensing or feeling and grappling with the language. And then I start to kind of shift between being a choreographer and a director and a facilitator, because then it seems the process shifts and the performers start to be given more particular tasks, and more opportunity to create material for themselves and to make decisions. So hopefully in those first couple of weeks I've set up the framework, and I've opened up the possibilities and set the premises of the language so that when people start making decisions, they're making decisions within the right framework.

So people then start to create material in response to their starting points and towards their scenes, so that when we then move on to the sites, when people start to go work in particular rooms or in particular spaces there is a concentration of language that is already in existence. So we have created this language and then we put it into a space, and then it's rediscovered and reinvented in relation to the sites.

And then there's a real shift in process, because it almost feels as if the luxury of looking at the body and looking at the language is kind of gone, because then you are looking at that element in context with the building, which is a formidable partner, actually, to start to work with. And it feels like the building, the building of the choreography or the physical language, and the dancers – and it's a complex little conundrum as to how all those partners work with each other.

When we arrive on site the first thing that we do – this is one of Felix's innovations – is to play a big game of hide and seek. That's where we send the performers into the building. The building ideally is dark, atmospheric, in a semi-state of design or transformation. And we send the performers in and just let them play in the building, and the direction is for them to absorb the atmosphere and to really allow themselves time to indulge their instincts in terms of space. So that exercise is not about creating material or making decisions, it's absolutely about indulging in existing in an empty building. Felix talks about – and it's actually really important – how those sensations and feelings that the performers get the first time they go into a building, that excitement, that energy, that fear, that curiosity, they are all of the emotions and the states that we are hoping to induce in our audience when they come into those buildings. So the performers need to really get that for themselves so that they can replay them and pass them out. So this game of hide and seek is really important, and we ask questions like, 'Where is your safe space? Where did you feel secure? Where did you feel uncomfortable?' and we set up some tasks in the space just to help provoke responses. We often do a tuning-up exercise before, where we remove the senses. Take away sight, focus on what people can hear, focus on textures and surfaces. It becomes a really sensory exploration. And that kind of brings us all together, so then at that point everyone is on a similar page. And it's quite a traumatic moment. It's very exciting, because you've got some language and you've got this great building, but it is really traumatic because the building feels immense and the performers get lost, and it feels completely impossible. That's probably essential to all of our work. I think if it didn't feel impossible we wouldn't be excited enough to take it on. It's when work feels really difficult – like the opera [*The Duchess of Malfi*, 2010] – that it becomes a huge challenge. And it's great for the performers because in a more conventional – I mean, this is a generalization – but in creating work for the stage a performer might just be on and off or in and out depending on their role. Whereas with our work the performers really craft their own show. There is no off-stage, you don't disappear off for a cup of tea half way through or go to the toilet. You create this character, and you tell these stories, and you stay with them throughout the whole of the performance. I think that gives the performer a real sense of ownership, and that's why I come back to this sense of the world that we create being inclusive and being nurturing, because everyone has to take responsibility for themselves within that and then create accordingly.

So when we are on site the process shifts, and it becomes more about making, and making decisions, often very quickly and very instinctively, about setting language, setting stories. One process is that we have this language that we brought into the site, and the particular task is to transpose that to a space. For example a duet that was made in the studio is transposed to a window ledge. That becomes the frame and the point of reference for that choreographic material. Another process is very much about creating in response to the building and the architecture. Another strategy is about the meetings that they have with the other performers during their journey around the space. They become the source or the starting point for something.

And then in our work we've always – or pretty much so far – created an ensemble event, sometimes two or three. They are kind of core to the ritual of the work and this idea that this experience is really fragmented and invisible and hiding behind corners and in nooks and crannies – and then from nowhere all of the characters converge and this little event happens. Our ensemble events are really structured and made and quite conventional in their concept. For example a party scene or a banquet.

How do the performers know when to go together to do one of these scenes?

All of their shows are structured and so they know within their structure that they will converge. It's not haphazard. They have a structure, they follow it, and at a certain point the structures collide and the big event happens. And that pulls audiences to one place. I find that part of our work really important, because there is something that I miss a little bit in creation in terms of not making so much work for the stage. One thing I really enjoy about theatre and dance when it's great is that moment of the shared experience when you are with other audience, and you have this amazing thing unfolding, often in front of you.

And I'm quite passionate that in our work the challenge is to have… The audience have this really individual experience, but to feel the kind of power and the dynamic and the surge of energy that happens when a crowd converges. You know, the power of the masses as opposed to the power of the individual. There are lots of nice tensions there. So these large ensemble events have become almost formulaic building blocks. They are there quite early on in our concept. In *Macbeth* [*Sleep No More*, 2003/2009] there was the banquet and that was a great opportunity to bring everyone together. Or there is a party. So hopefully the text that we are using offers those to us.

How do you choose the texts?

I don't know. How do you choose the text you choose? I think you are just drawn to them. I certainly have a list of texts and music that at some point in my creative life I'd like to look at and deal with. I think they sit on a little shelf and they bubble around and then certain texts offer themselves to you, they just pop up. They might have been asleep for a while, and you haven't thought about them for a few years, and then something will trigger them.

The first show we did was *Macbeth* [*Sleep No More*, 2003] and it was a play that I did in school and I just loved that play, and I knew that at some point in my life I would like to do something really interesting with it. So it was actually a big draw for me when Felix said, 'This is the play that I want to look at'. The next show that we did was *The Firebird Ball* [2005], which was based on *Romeo and Juliet*, because we felt it would be good to have still a classical text that the audience could grab onto, but something that had more of a lightness and more magic. The year after we did *Faust* [2006] because now it felt like the right time. I think we are drawn to these texts because they are very human, very expressionistic, rich in imagery – Shakespeare because it's poetry as opposed to prose. It's about texts that fire our imaginations and allow us to get rid of the language, actually. To look at the text and find the scenography.

When you are in the rehearsal studio, do you already have some kind of set design?

The process is always shifting. In terms of my dream way of working, I would love to have access to whatever came up in the moment so that the development of the design and the development of the choreography or the action is more synthesized, more synthetic. The design of the building, not completely, but in part, is pretty much decided before we start rehearsing. So that actually colours the improvisations. For example in *Faust* we'd have the sound, we knew the environment we wanted, we had a sense of the atmosphere, and we could feed that into the performers. Give them vivid descriptions of the places they were going to be inhabiting, and they would begin to play and create that world without the space, without the sets.

So the design and the sound are ready when rehearsals start?

The ideas are there and the materials are there. It's not by any sense done or fixed, but we've got a collection of sound sources when we begin rehearsals and things are fed in. And ideas of the building are there in terms of design. So we have a sense of where things might go.

The essential

What is the most important condition, in your opinion, to achieve a successful creation and rehearsal process?

We need the right company of artists; that's really important. And we do spend a long time making sure that we've got the right team together, both creative team and performing team. They are really simple things – time is essential, more time is always good. It's difficult if your rehearsal process is really pressured in terms of time, because just as pressure can sometimes create great ideas, sometimes it can kill them dead.

Boring, pragmatic things: we need a really good space, and support. It makes a lot of difference if there is good stage management support. I think everyone needs to commit to the idea and to agree to go on that journey, and everyone needs to go on pretty much the same journey, though people can take different routes and do little detours, but that shared journey towards a sensed destination or an impression of a destination is really important.

And how would you define a good team? What makes it a good team, or what is essential to have a good collaboration?

There's lots of things. There has to be a core level of trust running throughout. That's the basis. There has to be an energy, there has to be a sense of risk-taking and play. There has to be a kind of agreement in terms of the direction, although that doesn't mean everyone has to say yes to everything. It is not about saying yes, it is about asking the right kind of questions that are going to interrogate a process and an approach, rather than block it and stop it.

How do you deal with it when the process blocks? Do you have an example?

It's just painful, I think. I don't know. For us the process is most difficult when we open the show. Most theatre work is developing in previews

– that's what they are there for – but for us the previews are a whole new process because it's the first time that we see the audience in the building and moving around the building. And that's often when the show doesn't work, actually. It doesn't normally work for the first week or so, because we're having to navigate another level of performance, which is the audience as performer. They are completely free to roam so we are looking at the flow, the congestion. And performers then start to have to develop a whole language of signalling, when they realize that no one is following them to a scene or everyone is going that way… So there is a whole other language of gestural action, and the dynamics completely shift within the company. It's about the performers really understanding about pulling focus and shifting focus; it's about the creative team understanding where the sound runner drops out and needs to fill to pull a moment or where the lighting is too dark, so people aren't following. All of those systems of theatre need to be reworked to look at the building with an audience in it. Because the show looks great when you are walking around on your own in an empty building with performers. It's marvellous. But when you've got 200 people in the building it completely changes the energy.

I remember with *Faust*, all of us sitting in the bar on our second or third night. Audiences had ended up on the roof; they had ended up outside the building. We solved that, and then there was a whole other set of issues; the entrance wasn't working very well, and I remember we were all of us just sitting in the bar, scratching our heads till 2 o'clock in the morning, head down waiting, just batting around ideas and solutions and options until eventually somebody had an epiphany and we solved it. And not to blow our own trumpet, but we do pretty much solve everything. We are kind of relentless – sometimes to our detriment as individuals – but when we've got to work we have to make it work, all of us, and on so many different levels. And the performers solve so many of those problems themselves. They are real collaborators in that way.

What do you expect or look for in performers or dancers?

They have to be really skilled technically, whether that is as an actor or as a dancer. I think because I lead and drive the process we work more with dancers, and also because Felix's starting vision was about a language that is physical rather that text-based. The majority of our performers are dancers, but we do work with actors with a very particular sort of sensibility. Essentially we are looking for people who've got a really watchable… We always talk about their core presence or their ground state. You have to be able to fall in love with them as an audience. And that's not just about being good to look at; it's about having an energy and a charisma that kind of makes you superhuman. So we look for people that really stand out. And all of our performers have to be 'über-inventive'. They have to be able to create. They are all choreographers and makers within their own right. They have to be able to collaborate and not to be too insistent on their own vision or ideas, because we've had that in the past and that doesn't work. However brilliant somebody must be, they have to fall within these frames or parameters that we are setting. And actually, personality is really important, because people have to get on for a long time, so it goes back to that beginning phase of having tried to set up an environment where people want to go to work every day, and they want to give and they want to play and they want to enjoy.

Problems

Are there any recurrent problems, or what are typical challenges that you have experienced during the creative process?

Challenges. Well, there's loads of those. On a practical level, that shift from the studio to the sites. There is always a lot of tension, because you have come from a nurturing, safe environment and you potentially can move into areas of the building which are like building sites. It creates a lot of tension, because the performers want to create and make, and the designers need to create and make their work. So that's difficult. You want all elements of the production to be cared for, and nurtured, and have their sufficient time so that everyone can do their best work. That just sometimes doesn't happen, so that's challenging.

Cracking the idea sometimes is hard when you are devising, because you are taking the language away, you are trying to find the physical metaphor, find a different way of saying something. You're looking for that breakthrough.

Just working in a building brings a whole dimension of challenges. Because essentially you're making a theatre, or actually multiple theatres under one roof. Because there are so many singular stages existing, and they all have to have power so you can have light and sound. Making the building a safe space, a creative space, a designed space, a transformed space, and then a space in which you can hold an audience – it's a whole process of its own. Really, the bit that I do is the easy bit, and also the more conventional bit.

Dreams

What if anything was possible? What would you want to create, under what conditions?

It's about resources, time and resources, for me. Loads of time would be lovely. I'd love to have like sixteen weeks to make something.

I do have this dream where you would really be able to have a lovely synthesis between your technical team, your design team and your performers. We always talk about how we'd love to have a waterfall, we'd love to make it rain, we'd love to have snow… Our dream would be to have a studio transformed or a space where we could go and work for a week and play with all these weather factors and all these resources. Having all of those different ideas that we're touching upon in terms of technology, or design, or costume, having those resources at your fingertips. So you can just – as soon as an idea appears and you feel you really want to test it and play with it – that you can jump onto the idea and see if it's got any legs. So many brilliant ideas, I think, just go because they feel too impossible, too far away.

And having an ensemble. It would be lovely to give people that security as individuals just so they weren't worrying. Freelancing is so precarious. The security of a permanently funded group of individuals would be great. And a permanent space where we could live and... Well, not literally. I'm sure everyone says that.

We're taking my daughter now to lots of soft play areas and they're so great. I'd love to have one for grown-ups. Where everything is made out of foam and sponge and levels and slides and where you just climb and jump. I'd love that. I'd love a big soft play area. And a therapy centre [*laughs*]. Actually, creating in the context of a retreat for a period would be great, and I think we'll move towards that. It won't be for sixteen weeks, but we will move towards going out of London into the countryside at the beginning of rehearsal, to do some research. Because it just frees everyone up. It would be nice just to have everyone's focus and everyone's attention for the whole period, where your life isn't interrupted by ... living. Domestics. I mean, I couldn't do it for very long, I'm too old. Not hippie enough. But for a few weeks, a month maybe, I think it would be great. A little crèche for my children. A chef. That was really what we had at White Oak. You didn't have to think, you just had to get yourself dressed and brush your teeth in the morning and then go and be in the studio and work.

Interview: Deborah Vlaeymans

Maxine Doyle (UK)

Maxine Doyle (born 1970) is associate director and choreographer for Punchdrunk, with whom she has created a number of works since 2003. In Punchdrunk's performances the audience members are free to roam the performance site, which can be as large as a five-storey industrial warehouse, and can either follow the performers or simply explore the world of the performance.

Select works

Sleep No More (2003)
Faust (2006)
It Felt Like a Kiss (2009)
After Lethe (2016)

Website

www.punchdrunk.com

7

Jan Fabre

Why

Why did you choose to work in theatre or how did you end up in theatre?

I think it was love. As a young visual artist I did a lot of performance work. At the end of the 1970s, in museums and galleries. At one point I fell in love with a dancer, and later with an actress. I started writing for the actress – monologues. For the dancer I made a choreography. That's actually how my performance company started. Thirty years ago it was always dancers with actors. In a way I have trained dancers as actors to be with actors. So that everybody influences each other. I was a sort of a mediator between the different media.

How did you start making performance work in the galleries?

I went to two schools, The Royal Academy of Fine Arts and then in Cadixstraat [Antwerp] I went to the Municipal Institute of Decorative Arts and Crafts. There I attended the window display design line. And at a certain point, in my second or third year, I took the mannequins out of the window and I started working with my own body in the window, before I knew the word 'performance'. That's how I started making happenings with my own body.

Another important moment was when I was seventeen. I went to Bruges to see an exhibition of anonymous Flemish masters of painting. About self-inflicted stigmata. It was in 1977, and then I did my own first blood drawing, my first solo performance called *My Body, My Blood, My Landscape*. Since then I have done blood drawings every year, true to the Flemish art tradition. I discovered performance before I knew the words 'body art' or 'performance', through the classical

Figure 2 Deborah Vlaeymans and Jan Fabre, Antwerp, January 2009

Flemish paintings by the Old Masters. Combined with going to school, studying window display design, and taking the mannequins out of the window, and using my own body instead. That's how I started with my first performance.

Later, when I was twenty, I wrote my first text for the theatre. It was for one dancer and four actors and was called *Theatre Written with a K is a Tomcat* [*Theater geschreven met een K is een kater*, 1980]. And it came out of a kind of love – a curiosity to make something together with these people. I got arrested twice because of that performance. I was arrested in Belgium and in Chicago.

Did you go on working together with this ensemble?

No. After that we're in 1982. There I had auditions. Saw a lot of people. And I made an eight-hour long performance: *This is theatre as it was to be expected and foreseen* [*Het is theater zoals te verwachten en te voorzien was*, 1982]. In that performance there were a couple of performers who are still doing work, such as Marc Vanrunxt – who is a well-known choreographer – and Eric Raeves. They started with me. Els Deceukelier, with whom I worked for twenty years, Maria Martens, my dramaturg assistant, who is still working here at Troubleyn.

The third theatre production was *The Power of Theatrical Madness* [*De macht der theaterlijke dwaasheden,* 1984], in which Wim Vandekeybus started, and other actors who are also still working. Choreographers and directors. It was basic research, since the work processes lasted four, six to eight months. A foundation for my language. In these performances I took the experience of being a performance artist – the real time and action – into the codification of the theatre. That is actually the basis for my later theatrical research. Let's say the guideline. A practice that I have developed over the years and that I now teach to my ensemble.

How

How do you go from idea to product? Can you describe the process?

Let me take three different examples. *Requiem for a Metamorphosis* that I created in 2007 for the Salzburg Festival. It had eighteen characters. I wrote all of these down from beginning to end. That was, let's say, the starting point: my text. I also did a lot of sketches and models. I was really well prepared, but I still improvised quite a lot with my ensemble around the themes. It was about themes like butterflies, death and burial. Then there is *Orgy of Tolerance* [2009], the one I've just returned with from Chile and New York. Here all of the text is created together with the actors and dancers. It's a totally different kind of research.

I've just written a new text for Dirk Roofthooft. The third part of a trilogy, *The Servant of Beauty* [*De Dienaar van de Schoonheid*, 2010]. And this text has been written quite specifically for Dirk. Here every word is carefully discussed with the actor. But I also have a very clear vision of how I want to direct it. So these are three different types of work processes. *Orgy of Tolerance* is perhaps the most experimental and research-based process, because there are themes and I make sketches. There is a lot of physical and mental research. Explorations initiated together with the company. So the work process depends on what kind of production I am making.

Do you use a third eye or a test audience in these processes?

Nobody enters my work process. No, because I find that the actor and the dancer are so vulnerable mentally as well as physically. And we go so deep into the work that only people whom I have worked with for years can enter. I'm really talking about people who have worked for me for twenty-five, fifteen, ten years. And it's at a later stage of the process. For example just now in Chile we did six preview performances before going to New York to do the world premiere. These previews are like open rehearsals where changes happen every day; I cut things out or change something with the actors. So after five previews the performance looked 30 per cent different from the first. So yes, those I see as open rehearsals. But the work process is very closed. It happens rarely or never that somebody enters there. Because it really is a research laboratory, and it's very fragile.

So it varies in every process how much the performers are co-creative, but mostly you start with sketches or text?

Mostly it's text, drawings, and the next step is the models that I build. Models of the space and the place that I want to create. I do this with every production.

You make your own set design?

Yes, I make that myself and usually also the costumes together with someone, who sits next to me and who finishes the development and the making of the costumes. The lighting as well. I design that myself, but together with someone, the architect of this building [Troubleyn], Jan Dekeyser, who is a lighting designer and my architect. He looks at the ideas that I put down on paper. I give them to him and he realizes them technically.

And the music?

For example for *Requiem for a Metamorphosis* for the Salzburg Festival I invited Serge Verstockt, a composer I've known for twenty years, who has one of the most experimental music ensembles in Belgium, Champ d'Action. He created the music live during the work process itself. Composed it together with the actors and the dancers. It was also presented live. For *Orgy of Tolerance* Dag Taeldeman was the composer. He is from a well-known pop band in Belgium, A Brand. They've become very successful. With me Dag has created *As Long as the World Needs a Warrior's Soul* [2000] and also *Je suis sang* [2001]. Some of the actors, dancers or musicians who start with me may go on to become composers or pop musicians. And later on I ask them to come back here and compose the music for a production. They are closely involved in the creative process. That's always the deal. The composer must participate in everything. From morning till night. They even have to do research too. Improvise with the actors and the dancers so that they know the material from inside.

The essential

Can you remember a process that was very successful and why?

Actually there is no process that succeeds. You see, in the hardest moments, in the darkest and blackest days I see the most beautiful colour of rose. And that is why one does it. The days when I have … a kind of disgust with myself. When I'm disgusted with my own art. That is perhaps when the most interesting things come out. The days when I am against my own taste. The days when I … don't trust my actors and dancers. When I bring them in situations where they are on completely shaky ground. Those are the moments when the most interesting things happen.

Do you have an idea of how to create the shaky ground? What happens in that moment?

Listen, young lady, I'm… Actually, I'm a sneaky beast. I have prepared everything in the smallest detail before entering the rehearsal hall, and at the same time I play very naïve to the dancers and the actors, pretending that I don't know anything. If I close my eyes I know exactly what the production is going to look like. And during the work process I give them the feeling that they are inventing everything by themselves. Don't forget that in this democratic society being an artist, and in my case an artist and a theatre maker, makes you one of the last dictators. So I know very well what I don't want. Most of the time it's 'no, no, no, no, no', only now and then 'yes'.

Looking at it very concretely, what is for you essential for a successful work process?

That is very personal. In the last couple of years I've created really big productions such as *Je suis sang* [2001], *L'Histoire des larmes* [2005], *Requiem for a Metamorphosis* [2007], *Tannhäuser* [2004]. There have been forty to fifty performers involved. I've made a production again now – *Orgy of Tolerance* – with nine performers on stage. A work process of three months. What is nice about working with a small group of people is that there is no difference between working, going to a café, taking a break… Because it's an ongoing process. Breathing, or exploring, or challenging each other, making fun together, having a tough time together. What I enjoy is that the smaller the group the more intense it is. The more intimate it becomes. And it has been really fun that way during the latest process. But it's not a rule. You know, as an artist I try to cut off my own hands. Be against my own taste so as not to fall under a kind of system.

Can you imagine an ideal rehearsal process and what that would mean?

But that would be boring. What is the ideal work process? When everything is easy? That wouldn't be exciting.

So I guess a good result does not depend on a rehearsal process without problems?

No, on the contrary. Definitely on the contrary. Because I often place my performers in situations… What a performer reveals to him- or herself on a stage is not what you have directed. It's not how you have fed him or her. One of my great director role models is [Andrei] Tarkovsky. How he related to his actors. I have an enormous respect for my actors and dancers, but at the same time I try not to tell them too much about what I want to see. Because otherwise they will try to show that, play that for me. I would rather have them reveal things that they don't expect to show. That doesn't mean that if you have fun with your actors and dancers you will have a good work process or that you will make a good performance. Those things have nothing to do with each other. And certainly not when it comes to time, either. I've made performances in four days that were a so-called great success. I've made performances that I worked on for eight months that were, from the outside, so-called failures. Which is dubious. Success is a kind of poison. When is it a success? Because the reviews are good? Because it sells? It interests me very little, actually. Only as an artist can you… When is a work process or a production successful according to me? When I feel myself that I have started something new, that I have started exploring new things. When the work itself is teaching me something. When the work gives me something. When the work creates new questions for me, opens new doors. Then the work is good.

Problems

What is it more precisely that you don't want? What problems come up in the work process, maybe recurring problems?

But there are no problems. When there are no problems, there are no solutions. For me there is only a systematic choice of the investigation, the experiment. You see, I have been working for thirty years and I also try to train my actors, my performers. I always tell them – even though they have worked with me for ten or twenty years – I say to them, 'You may have built and deconstructed this wall more than thirty times, now build this wall again. But not from experience, from curiosity.' And that goes for me, too.

Dreams

Is there a method of rehearsal that you would like to try out, if anything was possible?

As far as I know I have for the last thirty years done all the things I needed to do for myself. There has never been a situation where I have censured myself. I think that my art works are free from any kind of ideology. It means that there is no moral judgement. I think this is true for me in theatre – not in performance art. When I've made performance art myself I've ended up in hospital several times. I've harmed myself. But I won't do that to others. To actors and dancers. I think actors and dancers should have a freedom, an individual freedom in my work process. So that they can develop themselves, so that their own body can be a target for them. So that their own bodies become a research laboratory for themselves. And I try to train my people so that they become their own director or choreographer. There must never be the feeling that you are commanding people. Because I believe that the most beautiful colour of a work process is the colour of freedom. Preparing a performance is like a… It's like preparing a battlefield of love. In sexuality between partners anything can happen, too, insofar as both parties agree.

Trust is essential?

I think so, yes. But of course you should ask my actors and dancers.

I *think* that some of these people have trust in me. But of course, you never know.

Any other thoughts on utopia?

I've got a lot of things on paper. I have started putting together a book called *Unrealized Projects*, and it is exactly about utopian projects. For example about painting the top of a mountain blue with a pen. There are a lot of projects that I know must stay unrealized. They are utopian projects. It's never about harming other people or hurting them or… Rather things that might – who knows – someday take place. Three years ago I didn't know I was going to do a big exhibition at the Louvre. Some things in life come to you. Right now I have big exhibition in Bregenz showing sculptural installations that I had put on paper in 1979. Only now have I been able to realize those ideas.

As I said, I would like to paint the top of a high mountain, the Mont Blanc, with a blue pen. For theatre there is an opening scene where I wanted to throw forty babies up into the air. I did it once with one baby, in 1982. I meet this woman sometimes now and she is twenty-five or twenty-seven years old. She has become a beautiful woman now. The one that I threw up into the air. But I wanted thirty or forty babies for that scene. So there are things that I have never done. Sketches. A drawing is a free space for the imagination. For drawing things that you might not be able to realize with real people. With me everything starts with a drawing.

Interview: Deborah Vlaeymans

Jan Fabre (BE)
Jan Fabre (born 1958) began his career in 1980 as director and stage designer. He made a clean break with the conventions of contemporary theatre by introducing the concept of *real-time performance*. The body in all its forms has been the subject of his investigations since the early 1980s. The name of Jan Fabre's company, Troubleyn, means 'remaining faithful'.

Select works
This is theatre as it was to be expected and foreseen (*Het is theater zoals te verwachten en te voorzien was*) (1982)
Je suis sang (2001)
Orgy Of Tolerance (2009)
Tragedy of a Friendship (2013)

Website
www.janfabre.be

8

Richard Foreman

Why

Why did you choose to make theatre?

Oh… I chose to do theatre when I was a young, young child. I started doing theatre when I was maybe nine years old. I was taken to see the Gilbert and Sullivan operettas – the English D'Oyly Carte [Opera] Company came to New York when I was around nine, and I was taken to see all of them. I went back to my grade school and started doing my own productions with my classmates. It began at that point and I just never stopped.

Because you thought it was fun?

No, I was very shy. It was a way to a content life. Where a shy person didn't have to be shy, because I had a fantasy world and I could tell people what to do. And also – just the suggestion of another world. My whole life I've never much liked the world I lived in. It was a kind of escape, I'm sure.

There is also another interesting answer, which you may not believe, but… When I was two years old they did a Christmas play. I was given one line; everybody in the class was given one line for the Christmas play. I was so shy that they took my line away from me. And I really – this was in the second grade – I said, 'I'm going to show them.' I just knew that I resented the thought that I couldn't be in this play, and I was going to do something about it. It really happened – and I really think that at that point I decided: I am going to show them that I can do theatre.

How

Can you describe your rehearsal process, from idea to product?

I always start with the text, in some way or another. Even though these days text is just collections, sort of fragmentary aphoristic phrases. But I start with that. And then I think about what is the central theme, and I start designing a set, make models. I usually go through nine or twelve models until I get something that seems right. Writing down, starting to collect music. So I have a selection of forty, or fifty, or seventy loops. And I have a set. Then I look at the pages that I have collected, and I just very casually make a list of possible props that might interact interestingly with what the text seems to say. And I end up with twenty or thirty pages. I go into rehearsal with that, and I just start on the very first day telling people what to do, just inventing off the top of my head things to do, combining, you know, 'Well, just try this prop, with this music, with these lines.' Of course, the process has changed a little bit the last couple of years, because for three years I did plays that had a filmed background. And that controlled things. I knew I was starting with the film. The film did not change in rehearsal. Everything else changed a great deal. Starting with the film helped determine what kind of setting I would choose, what kind of music, what kind of lines I was looking for. And now, I am going to do one more play next year with Willem Dafoe that is written more like a normal play. Much more text than usual. But that might be my last play for quite a while because I am moving into just making film.

Do you direct in the traditional way or is it more a common decision process?

Absolutely 100 per cent in the traditional way. I direct everything.

What about the set design and the music etc.?

I do all of that. We have the set set up on the first day of rehearsal. We have the music all arranged with the man having all the different possibilities of music. So from the first day I start telling people what to do, almost as if I was choreographing a dance. And I start trying out different music and in the course of the rehearsal, which is usually these later years something like fourteen weeks, the set gets repainted, gets changed, things get added, everything gets changed. I am making all those decisions.

The essential

What is in your experience the essential condition for a successful rehearsal period?

Successful rehearsal, well… I don't know, just that everybody gets along [*laughs*]. Since I am making all the decisions, you know, rehearsals… Some days it seems to be going terribly and I am depressed, other days it seems to be working. And I keep throwing out things and changing things. So it's very hard to answer that. Since it's not a – I mean it *is* a group effort in the sense that I depend on my performers, and I try to use people that I think are interesting. And I try to bring to the surface what I think I see as the most interesting thing in my performers. But I know that the rehearsal is going to go back and forth between seeming to go very well and then seeming not to go well. I make a lot of mistakes. It's part of the process.

What about the time, the place?

I have fourteen weeks, sometimes a little less. But the last couple of years, fourteen weeks. We rehearse six days a week, six hours a day and I just keep going through the play from the beginning again and again, and again and again. It's almost like editing a film. Seeing everything. At first, it's all done in a week and a half and I think, 'Wow, this is going to be pretty good, I don't know what we're going to do with all this rehearsal time.' Then we go back and do it again and I think, 'Oh my God, it's all awful.' And then I try to fix it and I think, now it's pretty good, and I look at it again and, *oh*, it's awful in a different way, and I keep going back over it. So it's the only thing that happens in rehearsal.

Do you think there is a connection between a good rehearsal and a good play?

I don't understand what a good rehearsal means. You are working towards something. You want it to seem intelligent and correct and somehow in harmony with my central obsessions so I just keep working to get to that point. Generally I have an internal clock and I know I have fourteen weeks and generally we are ready just about after fourteen weeks. It's a mysterious process. I work totally by intuition, not intellectually at all. Although in my other life I read a great deal and I write intellectual things, when I am making art it's all intuition and I never talk to the actors about theoretical or intellectual things. Just trust your intuition.

You are saying that you work intuitively, but you also said that you have the whole play in your head before the first rehearsal?

No, I have material. I have these phrases. I know I am going to change them. I know I am going to change the way they happen. I have a lot of music and I know that I am going to make a lot of bad choices at first as to which music I use where. Each page has a couple of props to be used in the staging but usually that gets changed. So I don't have the whole play in my head at all. I have a some sort of slightly incoherent vision of what I want to achieve. And then I just set up this arena which is the rehearsal space in which I keep changing things and trying to get them all to go together in the right way.

What about the costumes?

I usually work with a costume designer, but often I'll get up on stage and start using my scissors, changing the costumes and pinning it together in a different way. I give the costume designers little sketches of the kind of things that I want. It's all part of a big process of having a vague idea and changing it, and changing it. Sometimes the changes can be pretty radical.

Problems

What problem or situation do you never want to experience again, or what problems in the rehearsal process seem impossible to solve?

The only problem that I have never solved to my satisfaction is the treatment of the space between the front row of the audience and about the first two feet on stage. That is a very mysterious space to me. My audience always sits in front and watches, in the classical relationship, what's going on on stage. But that zone – it isn't energized for me, in a strange way. For that reason down through the years, sometimes I put a glass wall there that I write on, sometimes I put string in between. But that's really the only problem that I keep having. I think I come up with relative solutions, but it's the thing that always bothered me about the theatre. I don't think there are any other problems that I feel that I didn't solve, frankly. It's as if you are given all these elements and you just want to arrange them in a way that seems lucid, dense, intelligent in evoking some sort of spiritual intellectual realm. And that's always solved. You know I often say to my cast, 'The good thing about art' – and I believe it – 'is that in art there is *always* a solution'. It may drive you crazy trying to find it, but it's there. I think relatively speaking I have always found it for each play.

What about your relationship with your actors, set designer, musician…?

But wait, wait, wait! There is no set designer, there is no musician. I'm all those people. If you mean the person who is actually working with sound, well, he is a technician, who just starts the music that I select when I say start and so forth. Now I think I have a good working relationship with all these people. A lot of people seem to enjoy it and they come back more than once to do it. I'm not nasty to anybody. You know, sometimes I am sure it is a little boring for people because they have to sit there while I keep changing my mind again and again and again and again. But basically the rehearsals are pretty relaxed and I am not the kind of director who goes crazy and screams at people or anything like that.

I've been doing this for forty years and everybody knows about me and knows how I work. So people that get involved with me know what to expect. In the early days I had a few problems where actors didn't feel they were given enough freedom or they felt frustrated. But I always tried to frighten off, I tried to explain to people how I worked and told them, 'Look, this is the way it's going to be,' and there weren't too many problems. And back in France years ago, one actor told me, 'You know, Richard, it's very strange – you keep me in a narrow carter, and I'm not allowed to get out of that carter, but inside of that carter I feel freer than I ever have. Because you control so many things so carefully, but there are other, private things that you don't control, you let me be who I am.' I try with the actors to not have them play a character, but to bring who they are be totally present and available on the stage.

Dreams

What would you change or try out in the rehearsal process if anything was possible?

I believe that I worked very hard to set up a situation where I function in utopia. In America it's unheard of that people rehearse as long as I do, with the set, with the lights, with the sound from the beginning.

That is utopia, and I have it. The only additional utopia I suppose I'd like to be able to go to… I have worked in a lot of different countries. It would be nice if there were instant teleportation, so that I could do a play in Denmark or France and come back to my apartment in New York and go to sleep every night [*laughs*]. But the answer to my dream, my utopia, is that aside from having achieved that utopia in my theatre, I am giving up the theatre! I am moving into film and for me that is a move into what now represents a dream of beginning a new life, a new aesthetic life. It is a new beginning for me.

Why do you want to leave theatre for film?

I have always had a mixed feeling about the theatre. I have always hated many things about the theatre. My aesthetic interest at this point, all my ideas, I can only see realizing in film. Not because… Well, you can go out and film things outdoors and so on, and in theatre, I work only indoors in very limited settings. But just the matter of editing and combining all the levels of sound and image, and the way you can treat the image, the words and the way you can treat the words. I think the greater degree of control, the greater flexibility that exists in film is what I need now aesthetically.

It's almost as if in going to film also it's different because that problematic area is a thin zone. And actually, that thin zone is like the video or movie screen, where I'm now working. I am putting everything into that zone that I always found very problematic.

I'm seventy-one, and I'm beginning again! That's very exciting for me. Because all the things I hated about the theatre I can leave in the past [*laughs*]. I mean, someday I may do another play. I have to do a play next year, but after that I don't expect to.

Interview: Isabelle Reynaud

Richard Foreman (US)

Richard Foreman (born 1937) has written, designed and directed more than fifty performances in New York and internationally. His productions are characterized by a complex interchange between language, visual tableaux and a constant involvement of the audience. Foreman describes his work as 'total theatre'. In 1968 he founded The Ontological–Hysteric Theatre.

Select works

Symphony of Rats (1988)
My Head Was a Sledgehammer (1994)
Panic! (How to Be Happy) (2003)
Old-Fashioned Prostitutes (2013)

Website

www.ontological.com

9

Heiner Goebbels

Why

Why did you choose to work with theatre, or how did you end up in theatre?

Oh no, that would take too long… [*smiles*].

How

Can you describe your work process from idea to the final product?

What has been characteristic for all my projects since the beginning of the 1990s is that after roughly one year of conceptual approach I have at least two or three rehearsal periods. One rehearsal period about a year before the premiere, maybe a second one six months before the premiere, and then a third period to finish. What is also characteristic is that all these rehearsal periods must be done under real conditions. The light is not added in the end, for example, nor the ideas for the stage. I create everything simultaneously. Each project is very different from the others and the themes come from very different directions. Sometimes I start with a text, as for example for the performance *Eraritjaritajaka* with texts by Elias Canetti, which I had already known and reread for more than six years. Other plays start with a visual idea or the desire to work with a certain actor or a certain group of musicians. So there is always an initial motif, but it's characterized by a great deal of openness. I try to maintain this openness for a relatively long time, much to the regret of my collaborators, who naturally always want to know if this is how it's going to be. Usually it isn't, it changes even to the day of the last dress rehearsal.

It is important, however, that the relationship between the different elements and materials – the theatre media – is non-hierarchical. The text does not represent the first and most important law under which everything else is organized, nor is the music composed beforehand and then staying that way forever. Basically, all the media of the theatre – the lights, the space, the performers, the text, the music, the sound design – are developed simultaneously. And they are allowed to be made strong simultaneously by the artists that I am working with: stage designer, sound engineer, light designer, video or costume. This process is driven forward by the whole team together, as each of them tries to make his or her art strong. The light designer tries to make his territory strong and because he is there from the start, from the first rehearsal, or even before – and not just there in a conceptual way, but with lamps, moving things around, or saying, 'Let's do that again, I'll put up a light here from behind' – all these things can be brought together. Because my most important experience in theatre is that everything that is added subsequently will only have an illustrative role. It can only acquire a structural meaning if it is there from the beginning. If you are working with an actor who has already learnt the text with all the parts of his body, and you say, 'Now we add the music and it will interrupt you here and here,' then of course he will protest and his body can't react to it anymore. There is a gravity of what he has learnt. If you are trying to work with music and text in an equal balance, like I do, then you have to do it from day one. And any resistance coming from the other media, like the music or the lights or the space, makes the actor even stronger in the end.

The essential

The condition is a rehearsal process that stretches over a long period of time and where I have all the 'instruments' from the first day. I know that's very luxurious, and I don't know anywhere in Germany where I can rehearse like that. I can do it in the theatre that I've collaborated with for the last ten years, Théâtre Vidy in Lausanne in Switzerland.

And the third condition is a theatre that makes their space, their mechanics, their technique, their resources available to me as an unconditional laboratory. I need a theatre that doesn't say to me, 'You have to take these ten actors,' or 'You have to take this orchestra,' or 'You have to take these singers.' When I begin a project I need to be able to choose all these elements freely, including the performers, including the musicians. Choose exactly the right people for the right project.

In *Hashirigaki*, a piece I created in 2000, I chose a Swedish performer, a Canadian and a Japanese musician, and even though the director of the theatre had serious doubts about their availability at first, we ended up doing more than one hundred performances around the world, from Australia to Hong Kong, from New York to San Francisco and of course in Europe. It worked very well for nearly ten years. This experience proves that you can produce theatre beyond the repertoire practice that is the rule in Germany. When you can set up a piece without interruption, not just arriving on stage at three o'clock in the afternoon, but maybe developing for two, three days and then showing the piece ensuite for a week, then of course you can be much more precise with all the details. You can really make use of the space; you can use the light and sound systems on a completely different level. The constant flexibility of the technical level which is demanded by the repertoire productions can only work with an enormous division of labour. But it means that the individual technician has no overview over what is going on.

For my projects it is essential that the sound and light technicians are there from the first rehearsal to the end, there is no change of shift. They are irreplaceable, like the actors themselves. They might be there from nine in the morning to eleven in the evening, and during the night they think of new solutions. They are highly motivated, responsible and very constructive, creative individuals in this process and not interchangeable shift workers who just provide, so to speak. That is another very important part of the production.

I have just made a piece called *Stifter's Things* [*Stifters Dinge*] that premiered last September [2007] and is now on a long tour. It is a performance without any cast, no actors, no musicians, no dancers, no singers, no performers. It's a performance basically consisting of stage elements: of light, water, fog, rain, ice, projections, sounds (metal sounds, stone sounds) and five pianos that play mechanically. This piece would of course have been impossible in a normal theatre. I wanted to develop a piece that was based on exactly the absence of what you would normally, and traditionally, define as intensity and presence in the theatre. And I wanted to create a work in which the spectator is the sovereign, the irritated sovereign – in the centre of perception. That was possible in this theatre in Switzerland, because when I said to the director, 'In my next piece I don't need any actors,' he said, 'Okay, then I won't hire any.' Instead, I needed a really good programmer and musical assistance and five self-playing pianos, and that was not a problem. And that's how a production should be that is truly experimental, where you don't know beforehand what will be the result in the end.

This is characteristic of my processes. I don't have any visions of a piece that are in any way representative of what is actually created in the end. I instigate a procedure, a process. I know what I don't want to do, I know what the task is or what my interest is or what my questions are. And then together with a team I invent something that I couldn't have imagined myself beforehand. I find that this is the only possible way in which you can make theatre as an experiment. You cannot avoid the traps of convention if you work within the routine of a repertoire production and its expectations.

What is the advantage of dividing the rehearsals into three periods?

I need time for errors. Firstly because I don't know what a piece is going to be like later on, and secondly because during the process I never imagine anything as 'finished' and then try to enforce it at all costs and perhaps against the potential of a performer or a space – on the contrary I want to discover something. I also want to discover something in the performers that I don't know yet, that they might not know yet. For example, I work with excellent musicians and I don't give them a score, because I know already that they can play anything. Instead, I give them texts or tennis balls or instruments that they've never learnt to play, to find out what else these musicians can do. In this way I create a piece in which the musicians grow beyond their abilities, become performers and not just an orchestra.

The most important thing about the first phase is that it is a completely open, an experimenting improvisation, about the cast, or the space, or the texts, the potential topics. In the second phase – if there is one, sometimes the second phase is already the third – I try to focus the rehearsal more on a possible structure for the coming piece. Then I know what material and which texts will not be included, and which musician might be suited for this costume, what has to be built etc. In the first phase I have often worked with dummy texts, not with texts that will go into the piece later on, but any kind – texts about gardening or texts from an art history book. And not until later have I found the texts that I actually need for the project. In the beginning I still might not know exactly who is able to speak. When I'm not working with actors, first I have to find out who can actually speak and if they can, which language would be better, Hindu perhaps, or French or Spanish? The first phase is an experimental research for the possibilities sleeping here that I am still not aware of. If we ignore the conventional hierarchy of the theatrical elements, we need time to observe their relations, their influence on each other. It is a research.

Do you think that the better the rehearsal process is, the better the performance will be?

I believe very strongly that when seeing a performance you can sense how it has been created. Georg Seesslen, a film critic and researcher, has made a formula for this: since film and above all theatre is a social process you can tell from a production whether the director is an asshole or not. Whether he treats his actors as objects, pushing them from here to there, or whether they are conscious, self-reliantly acting subjects that are involved in the process of creation. And you can enlarge that in the sense that you also see how he relates to the technicians or to the other forces: space, light, sound. Whether he is impatient, authoritative and hierarchical, or whether he has a playful relationship, allowing the light to suddenly become more important than the performers, because it expresses something about the theme in a better way. You can see all that in a production, and I think that a lot of the luck or the success that I've had with my performances during the last ten years is above all due to a creative and often collective production method. A non-alienating work method in which everybody has a voice is the most important thing.

Problems

Is there a problem in the rehearsal period that always seems to come up and that you don't really have a solution for?

No, for me there isn't, because I have promised myself not to work under certain compromising conditions anymore. I only work with teams that I've already known for years, and in a theatre with which I have had positive and open experiences in the past. I get a lot of requests – for instance commissions for operas from opera houses – but I never accept them. I know that the institutional form of an opera production would force me to make so many compromises that I couldn't do it well. I wouldn't be good at it. So I don't accept them and therefore I sleep well at night. Mostly. If not, it's my own artistic problem. It's not an institutional resistance, so to speak. Once you have worked in a municipal theatre or opera house, which I did very often in the 1980s as a composer for other directors, you know how much energy is swallowed up by institutional restrictions, resistances and union problems. In 2005, I directed one of my own orchestral cycles at the Venice Opera La Fenice; it was a truly horrible and unbearable experience with regard to the working conditions, the schedules and the restrictions that the musicians have imposed upon themselves through their union agreements. I'm not going to repeat that ever again.

If you experience a personal artistic block, what do you do to solve it?

You can minimize blocks when you work in teams. Blocks are mostly somehow hardenings or isolations, and when you have worked with your set designer or your sound technician for twenty or thirty years, then you don't have to be the only 'inventor' of a performance. The solution can very well come from somewhere else, from where you don't expect it. When you have accepted that you don't have to find everything yourself, life becomes a lot simpler.

Dreams

If anything was possible, what would be your absolute utopia?

In general, I don't have any utopias at all. I work in reaction to a given. I mainly work with commissions and not because I have an 'idea' or an existential need of my own. I find ideas dangerous. Theatre should not be about the imagination of a director. Theatre should be creating a space in which the imagination of the audience can take place. But mostly what you see in theatre is the opposite: that the set designer, or the costume designer, or the director has had too many ideas, and the spectator's gaze is blocked. There is nothing left to discover, it's all imposed on you. Every possible thing is shown. I'm more interested in withdrawing myself and opening up mental spaces for the audience. Spaces to make their own discoveries, spaces for their own imaginations. And that's why I don't have any utopias, none at all.

Interview: Isabelle Reynaud

Heiner Goebbels (DE)

Heiner Goebbels (born 1952) is a composer and director. His work has toured extensively and has given a new dimension to the concept Gesamtkunstwerk. He presents a number of ingredients and it is up to the spectator to sort them. Heiner Goebbels is professor at the Institute for Applied Theatre Studies at the Justus-Liebig University in Giessen and president of the Theatre Academy Hessen.

Select works

Der Mann im Fahrstuhl (1987)
Schwarz auf Weiss (1996)
Stifters Dinge (2007)
Louis Andriessen: De Materie (2014)

Website

www.heinergoebbels.com

10

Helgard Haug

Why

Why did you choose to work with theatre?

I started with a very classic fascination of theatre. Already in school, with the theatre society and going to see theatre. I tried to find out as much as possible about the work behind the scenes, until I finished my A-levels. And I've always thought that it was a career or a field that you could look at or approach from many different sides. I was also always very interested in visual arts and thought that I would go the way of stage and space design and so on. I also had a fascination of texts and what you can do on stage, and so I started studying theatre – Applied Theatre Science [Angewandte Theaterwissenschaft, University of Giessen]. And at first, the studies took me a long way away from that. Because they questioned what comes from a playing impulse or maybe a naïve impulse, what makes you burn. Consequently, at the end of the studies I didn't want any more to do with theatre. Instead I focused on installation – and the projects that I had done during my studies became more and more visual and turned towards installation works, media works. But then I felt the lack, when suddenly you're only working in galleries or for the radio, of communication with other people, collaborators but also an audience. And I started considering if some of the questions I had should be moved back into theatre to be discussed there. So first it was a naïve approach, then the shock of the fundamental questioning, and finally the chance that I had understood what it means when people come together in a room; what it means when you're with an audience for two hours to focus on a certain question, certain people, certain lives or certain texts. You could say that's how I came back to it.

What was the main reason that you turned away from theatre for a while after your studies?

The question was, where can I make theatre at all? Everything that was institutional theatre I found highly suspicious. The vanity didn't interest me. The questions that were dealt with in the theatres at that time, the very self-reflecting, self-absorbed, didn't interest me. I was revolted by the way people behaved around each other there. When you walked into a canteen at a theatre and heard how the actors ordered a coffee, it was so artificial, so revolting to me that I thought, I never want to end up there. And I couldn't imagine how I could make theatre without working in an institution like that.

Then we started making our own projects, and they also took us a long way away from what theatre normally is. We always tried to extend them or do them differently. Being on stage in a different way, performing ourselves. Doing anything but what is done in a normal or classic way.

How

Can you describe your work process from idea to product?

One of the reasons why I've stayed with theatre is perhaps that the projects are so different. And I can't say that this or this is a typical way of generating a theatre project. The plays are very different, have very different structures and therefore also different methods. To differentiate ourselves from what happens in normal or narrative theatre we used to describe it by saying it's like the difference between a fictional film and a documentary. So it could be called documentary theatre, only I find that definition a bit too simple.

But it means that we have to research the themes for our projects, and that even though we work together as a team we have to agree on a certain theme beforehand. We might get an invitation from somewhere, Copenhagen, saying we'd like you to create a piece for our city, or for this festival or for this place, and then typically we go there and observe. We spend time there, and maybe we have brought a theme that has caught our interest or fascination in another context. We start talking to people and looking for a possible structure. Is it a performance that takes place on the stage, should it tour, can it be an intervention? Is it something that we will make only once in this place and never again? Can it involve another kind of communication, like for example, a piece we made between India and Germany [*Call Cutta in a Box*, 2008]? Where people call each other and don't even share the same theatre space.

We always find content and form, really, by approaching this city or these people. We just spent a week in Istanbul, and we said we wanted to meet people from this or this field, and all during the meetings and the talks the engine keeps running, and the questions: how can this help us, where can this lead us, what is the next step? Do we need a counter impulse or someone from a totally different field? For example here we met a lot of people who practice boxing. It's a new trend in Istanbul, but quite an old trend here in Germany. The Turkish people in Germany, or people of Turkish origin, are very active in boxing. There are thirty-two boxing clubs and many of them are used and run by Turkish people. We wanted to transfer that to Istanbul, and they said, 'Forget it, boxing isn't a theme here at all, it has nothing to do with Istanbul.' But we found a boxing club for professionals, where they have a national team and a national training programme. And we just started talking to people: Why do you box? What kind of meeting is that?

We keep looking; it's very focused on research. At some point we find the protagonists and decide who will be in the play, if it's a play for the stage, and we start rehearsing. The rehearsals are a relatively short period in proportion to the development of the entire piece. The research, the travelling, the talks are very, very long, and then we rehearse maybe four weeks or so. When we meet the audience for the first time, mostly the piece isn't finished. We gather experience and keep working between every showing. Many of the pieces tour, and with every new place we can test what works here. Add a new impulse or make cuts. Mostly we have much too much material so we cut it down to an hour and a half and then continue working on it. It's a never-ending process.

When you have rehearsals, what are they like? Do you have a concept for the process?

There is a reason why we invite the specific people, something that we have found out during the talks. A fascination for something they do or for the way they see the world. Or their form of theatre perhaps, that they have in their own reality. A biographical aspect that interests us. First we work at the table. We say, 'Tell me the story again,' or we ask questions. Then we try out different set-ups on stage, sometimes spatial things like a revolving stage. We try out lots of things. Often we rehearse separately, since we are two or three directors – that means we rehearse individually with people or develop something with someone, and then we try to construct a structure. We'll make an initial sequence with four or five ideas or scenes and look at it. Does it work, does the structural principle work, do we need to try something completely different?

There is often a big spatial set-up, like the placement of the audience or the way the stage is set, or a technical thing. Maybe the participants have to operate certain techniques, for example projections. We just did a piece in Vancouver [*Best Before*, 2010] about computer games, where the protagonists were more or less hosts for the 200 people in the audience who could then play computer games themselves. The formal framework and the set-up of the play is built up layer by layer based on what the participants tell us.

Is the text always fixed or does that vary?

The text is written, and it really always goes through our pen. Things that people have told us, and sometimes we want to sharpen it. Or we insert particular statements in the text that the person has never said, or that they will disagree with and have to handle. We also include things we've found during the research period. They are real, written plays. And then of course in the performances the important thing is that they say it in a natural way. That they liberate themselves from it, so that it's not about where the sentence ends or begins, but that they communicate as directly as possible. That they are present on stage and aware of what they are saying, using their own words but within a structure that we have made for them. They mustn't recite, that's the worst. When you feel that they have become machines saying a text, and of course they will do it poorly compared to an actor. The advantage and the reason why we say that they are experts is that you know that what they are saying comes originally from them, and you can enrich it and shape it, which is what we do. But the most important thing is that they say 'I' and mean themselves, and it is not a recited I, or an artistic I, or an imposed I. But it's something that you have to remind them of during rehearsals when they have repeated a story five times and they are thinking, 'Why the hell am I saying this for the fifth time, haven't they heard me?' It's the perverse thing about theatre, the incessant repetition. I'm saying it here and now, but tomorrow I have to say it again, and we have to work hard to keep it alive. They have to keep up the enthusiasm and the interest in the repetition.

How do you do that?

We make them conscious of the situation. There are always new spectators, so the story that you're telling is also always new. You're not telling it to the lights, even though they may be blinding you. You have to understand that behind it there are people who don't know anything yet, and who have come with expectations of this evening. We also change things shortly before the performances. We have a routine where the participants arrive an hour and a half before, and we tell them to change something or decide a change together. In plays about day-to-day subjects we can insert new content, small passages, and thereby keep the performance alive.

You work all three as directors and writers on a piece?

Yes, we work in different constellations, but Rimini Protokoll is three people: Daniel Wetzel, Stefan Kaegi and me. When we have parallel rehearsals, we each withdraw with different people for an hour or so, and we try to really understand a piece of text, or maybe we have prepared it for this rehearsal. We rehearse it with the protagonists, specific ideas and actions. After a while we meet and look at all of it together. We decide what should be the first part etcetera, and then we watch it as a sequence.

We work together, because our heads are different and we find our differences interesting. We discuss a lot and we try out a lot. There are three different forces working on it. And in a given moment I may not find it absolutely wonderful, because maybe I'm thinking that I'm at another point or I want something different, but the difference keeps us together. We have three different ways of grasping things, which is good, and the participants also come at us in different ways. Maybe I don't work well with this person, but then Daniel does. We can divide the work and complement each other. Nevertheless there will of course be a piece that we have written together. Where we really build on each other. One evening I will finish writing it, then Daniel reads it and restructures it, and then it goes to Stefan, who will add something. But of course we also often make projects that are interventions and not traditionally rehearsed plays.

Which process of creation have you experienced as the best one and why?

I don't think I can say. We always have the feeling that there is too little time. I suppose that's how it is, the opening date is getting closer and you're thinking, 'Now I know what this is all about and now I really should have had three more weeks,' or, 'Now we should rethink something from the very beginning.' That feeling is always there, and at the same time I like working towards that point. Knowing that shortly before the opening and in all the tension, suddenly there is so much that you are able to see and understand and change. Working towards that point when the opening really is the first real moment that you have with the piece. Even though you've had the dress rehearsal and maybe invited people to see it and you've got a sense of what it is.

It's always the first thing that comes to my mind when I think about the not ideal: the feeling that there is too little time. And at the same time I think that such a process must have a certain duration. Also because the people we work with have normal jobs that they've taken time off from. They've had to reorganize their lives, set aside their hobbies, neglect their partners or families to concentrate completely on this process for a short time, and you can't extend that forever.

Can you think of an example of a good rehearsal process?

Up to a certain point we've always refused to work with prewritten texts. We've said, the texts come from these people and we confront them with dramaturgies that interest us. And often theatre directors and dramaturgs asked us, 'What would you do with a classical text in a project?' Then there was the International Schiller-Days [2005] and we took *Wallenstein*, the dramatic text, and we decided to overwrite it with biographies of persons who were not from theatre. We stayed with the dramaturgy of Schiller's text, and that was sort of an eye-opener to me. I realized how great it was to be able to take an existing dramaturgy and use it. Work within a canon where the audience comes with a knowledge of the text and the classical dramaturgy, and you are able to contribute something to it. The work process was not at all ideal, but the step in itself was ideal, and it opened up a new field for us. It's not a no-go zone anymore, but a field in which we can work and which we can use to expand our form and approach.

Is there a connection between the final product and the rehearsal process? Is it possible to say that the better the rehearsal process the better the performance?

An interesting question. I don't think so. I think what you would like to have is a frictionless or trusting relation with the participants, but then again trust is something else. The pieces in which we've had the toughest conflicts with the protagonists have often become the best. Although during the work you wished yourself far away, and developing the material was very laborious. The process is often not so ideal and involves a lot of discussions and setbacks. Paths that you have to go along ten times before getting to where you wanted to go. And maybe the result is good and maybe that's because of the discussion you had. But while you're making it you curse it all and think, 'Can't you just say what I've written here? Why is that so difficult?'

Das Kapital [*Karl Marx: Capital, Volume One*, 2006], for instance, was a piece that caused an insane amount of discussion, and where we fought a lot of scepticism and headwind, because the participants didn't believe that you could make a theatre piece of that text. It was too much, impossible – and we wanted to work with people who enjoyed trying to prove our point and at the same time putting it into question. It was troublesome, costly and incredibly nerve-racking, but at the end somehow a piece came out of it that I like very much, and I don't think you see all the trouble in the piece. You can see that it's a difficult text to work with, but the participants are very open and enthusiastic in the performances.

The essential

What are the essential conditions for achieving the result that you want?

A good team is essential – I mean local people. Very often we don't work in Berlin and we need a good team on the spot. People who do research and communicate with us for a long time beforehand.

If it's a play I always like to rehearse in the performance space, because then we can really build up something over time. For example, with *Wallenstein* we knew that we had the space for six weeks, and that was really ideal. We were also able to do our own work there, writing and meeting people, and then going slowly into staging and rehearsing. Then there wasn't this moment where everything is suddenly upended. In our experience it's often difficult for people who are not used to theatre: to suddenly be in this space with all the empty chairs, and to suddenly get a notion and a fright of what's coming and what they've gotten themselves into. And the machinery seizes you, the lights come on, and all the technicians and all the other people assisting are suddenly there to grab hold of you. So it's great when it's a space that you can slowly warm up, so to speak.

What is essential in your collaboration?

Patience, perhaps. Again, that has something to do with time. We often work on several projects at the same time. Then the question is: How much time am I giving to each project? How patient am I? or How fast do I want to move on with it? There are different phases that we go through – sometimes we all want to do something else. Then maybe you're a bit tired, or self-critical or impatient. And sometimes it's really relaxing and you get good work done.

I'm always curious of what forms or new challenges will come up. It's of course different whether I'm working in Canada or Turkey. We have to react to so many things and work through them, because we do everything ourselves, in fact – from negotiating contracts to checking out rehearsal spaces, everything. It's essential that everything is in order and that there is support from the theatre or the festival, also financial.

And the questions are essential. How am I touched by the questions of a piece? How does it have something to do with my life, or where is a research taking me? Where can I find a theme that questions me or brings me further or brings my life further, or what is an important theme for this place?

Problems

What is the biggest problem that you have had in a rehearsal process? Or, what problem have you still not found a solution for?

There is something that happens often and that we haven't solved yet. We often experience that people tell us something that later on they don't want to say on stage. We might also say: 'Don't tell this story on stage,' because we know it's dangerous or risky, or it's just too private. But there is the other way round, where we find people whom we think have something very important to tell. And in the beginning they agree, and we rehearse, and then comes the point where they say, 'No, I'm not going to say this after all,' because they are afraid of the public, of legal consequences, of their parents, whatever.

It happened once in Vienna when we were doing a piece about diplomacy. They had really told us some great stuff, but then the piece became very difficult because at each rehearsal they were backtracking. And suddenly it became clear that that's exactly what diplomacy is, that you don't say things as they are, there is always a kind of: Yes, it could be like this or like that: how I say it depends on who I'm talking to. And you can't just say certain things to an audience. So the things that had a certain starkness or where you could perceive a certain extremeness of political attitude just became harmless, because they kept backtracking. We've also experienced it recently with a piece about Vietnamese people living in the Czech Republic and Eastern Germany, about the trafficking routes that they use to get to Prague [*Vùng Biên Giói*, 2009]. They told us a lot of things, and a lot of them said, 'It's no problem to tell you this, we have a status now where it isn't dangerous anymore.' But then the fear of their own community grew so big that they wouldn't tell us anything anymore and wouldn't participate at all. It's tragic. When you feel that you've have found a good way of working and you're ready to perform the piece, and somebody suddenly drops out.

Dreams

What would you like to try out if anything was possible?

At the moment I am preoccupied with people who have left the earth – I mean space travel. In 2013, there's a German who will be sent into space, and I have just tried to arrange a meeting with him, but they protect those who are in the training programme. I've been looking at the first images from the first trip to the moon again and again, and I think it's incredibly fascinating. I would love to work with people who go so far away from this here and now, from time, and who take on such a risk. To fly with them would be utopian, I mean, ultimately I think I would do it. But exactly this, to ask yourself what kind of courage that would take. Will you come back? Will you make it? Do you want to come back? What is life like when you have been so far away? I find that only when you've been abroad there are these questions of what life is like when you come back, what has changed, and what have you come back to?

It's very personal, I'm just completely fascinated by the subject. I'm interested in the impulse, the countdown and the moment that you take off. Also this funny search for another kind of life that might be up there. The amount of energy and money that's being poured into something going away from here; you could argue that our world has enough problems, why don't we spend our money to solve them first before we indulge in the luxury of going into space? But it's a primal longing, I think, to see what lies behind, or what's this moon like, that shines so beautifully at night? Can you make footprints on it? Should you ram a flag into it, or what kind of absurdity is that? I am totally fascinated by the persons who work towards this and who are able to keep and realize their childhood dream of becoming an astronaut. Perhaps I would build a theatre on the moon, or hang up a stage curtain. A curtain that doesn't wave.

I have written a kind of manifesto that poses the question: Where – at all – can you make theatre? How can you use a location to its fullest? What if a whole city was involved? How could I communicate it? A fellow student of us once did something like that in Giessen. They interchanged day to night and tried to get as many people as possible to go to sleep at noon, and mow the lawn or go to see the public authorities at night. People got married at night, some of the shops participated – so in a small town you could somehow reach people and communicate it. But how could you transfer that to a monster like

Berlin? And communicate to the three and a half million people living here so that they are all part of it and aware of being part of a staging, a performance? That would be great.

Interview: Isabelle Reynaud

Helgard Haug (DE)

Helgard Haug (born 1969) is director and concept developer in the performance group Rimini Protokoll that creates performances for the stage, the urban space and for radio with the participation of 'experts' instead of actors. Besides Helgard Haug, Rimini Protokoll consists of Stefan Kaegi and Daniel Wetzel. The group has been the founder of a new international reality trend, winning a series of international awards.

Select works

Call Cutta in a Box (2008)
100% Stadt (2010)
Situation Rooms (2013)
Adolf Hitler: Mein Kampf, Band 1&2 (2016)

Website

www.rimini-protokoll.de

11

Bojan Jablanovec

Why

Tell me how you ended up in theatre.

Before I went to the theatre studies in Ljubljana, I went to the School of Economics, because my parents were not sure it was a good idea with theatre, and I decided to follow their advice. They said to me, 'You need some kind of profession and this is not a profession'. At the School of Economics I immediately gathered a group of people who were interested in theatre and I started to do theatre there [*laughs*], which was quite weird. We did it for three years. Then I decided that I had to do it for real. And everything developed into the professional world of theatre.

But somewhere along the way you changed your approach to theatre?

Yes. My story is connected to the institutions. Obviously in the beginning everybody dreams about working in the theatre, on the stages, with the actors. I was a good student at the academy, and pretty soon I started to direct in the national institutions in Slovenia. They recognized me as a talented young director. They also awarded me. And it became harder and harder for me, because my ideas were stuck and I couldn't break through with them in this kind of institutional way of working. My performances became more and more weird for the general audience, and they started asking themselves, 'What is happening with this young director? What is he doing? He is so talented. What's wrong with him?'

I realized that I had to do something, because this was going nowhere, I was not satisfied and people around me were not satisfied.

I was always trying to push something, but I didn't really know what I was fighting. Then I realized that I was fighting the production system – it didn't work for me. I simply cannot fit into it. I decided to make a radical cut and not to have anything to do with them anymore. So I refused all offers of work. This happened while I was an assistant lecturer at the Academy of Acting in Ljubljana. I was watching the process from the other side, because before I was a student, and now I was the assistant of an older professor. I could not understand why some people are put into a situation where they are supposed to know so much about how theatre should be done and what it is about. And to lecture young people who are really hungry for knowledge. They were teaching them something that I didn't believe in from the beginning. And now, after ten years of experience I realized that this logic didn't work for me.

I decided that you have to build your own production logic where you can fit in, and then try to develop this logic somehow. Find your own way. I didn't know from the beginning what my way is, and what I would actually like to do and how I would like to do it. I just knew what I hated. So I started from what I didn't like. This and this and this – I didn't like anything. I knew a lot about what I didn't like. That was good. I thought if you just go through the things that you don't like, you will find something that you like. So *Via Negativa* started. This was a way. Through what you don't like, you will discover something that you like. And this thing that you like, sooner or later you will find out what you don't like about it – and in this way maybe you can improve your way of thinking, doing, creating. This has now basically become a process of working.

How

Can you describe it in more detail? What is the typical Via Negativa *process?*

It's really simple. Usually we start with a theme that I bring. Basically, in the beginning of *Via Negativa*, in 2002, I was aware that a theme is important, because it's a kind of subject that holds people together, to think about the same subject. But more important is *why* they are doing it, so that is the second big question. What? Why? And the third big question is: How? I didn't know how to do it. My answer to 'What' was, 'Because I don't like it the other ways.' I didn't know what the subject should be. And because I was practising this negative selection, I said, 'Okay, let's do a series of performances on seven related themes. The basic negative qualities in the civilization, in human lives, in individuals, that we have to fight with. To find a kind of material that has conflict in itself. A kind of material that everyone can connect with. A personal subject somehow.' I started to collect people with the question, 'Would you be interested in doing something about anger? I would like to find an interesting way of doing it, so we will learn from each other, me from you, you from me, and we will somehow develop this work.'

We started developing the work, and after two or three years I had a little method for how to work and how to find results that we were all satisfied with. It is really simple. I don't like rehearsals in the common sense of the word, where you repeat something in order to improve your ability to do a situation you already *know*. We have rehearsals where it's always a kind of small performance: We agree to think about a subject and the following week you show us your own little piece about it, and we will look at it and be your audience. The only thing we know about it is that it is about greed, so we have a general idea of what you are talking about, but we don't know specifically what you are talking about. You be quiet about it and just show us the piece.

The performer comes and shows his or her piece; we watch it and then we react to it. We tell him what we saw, how we understand it, what our associations were about it, and if maybe we have any suggestions for him. Or we just react in a simple way, 'I don't understand it at all,' or, 'It was boring,' or, 'Yes, it's funny, but I don't know why it's funny,' or, 'It's weird,' or, 'It's nice'. We are trying to find answers to why it is nice or interesting for us as spectators.

I just ask the performer to listen to us, select the opinions that he found interesting and find his own answers to the reactions that we gave him. Next week he brings a new idea. Maybe he decides to do something completely different, because he saw last week that he was completely misunderstood. From our reactions he can learn how we view and understand his showing. This is the process that we repeat week after week, month after month, until we understand each other. We slowly learn from each other.

Now, the process is a little faster with people who work with *Via Negativa* regularly, and even people who come for the first time can also learn fast, because we have become more experienced spectators. We can react more precisely on what we see. This work we develop until we are no longer satisfied with the small pieces. Then I take the responsibility of thinking about the context of the work, the basic structure, focus, how to lead the spectators, how to see the pieces, or how to build a structure where all these stories or actions on the stage will find a proper place in order to be effective and understood in the way that the performers wanted.

The next and final step of rehearsal is the performances, the meeting with the audience. The first moment where we can see how the exchange has worked. And then we just develop the work. The performance *Casablanca Therapy* [2010] here in Aarhus was the third version of this piece.

And do you get verbal feedback from the audience?

Sometimes you talk to people, but for me, the most precious moment is while the performance is going on. It's not even necessary to look at the audience, just to feel how it's working. I don't understand why this always happens to me, but when I am sitting with the audience during the performance, I see the performance completely differently than while I am making it, and I bang my head and think, 'Yes, of course.' Then you change things and of course, that opens new problems in the structure and you just have to tune it, until you don't know how to do it better, and then you can leave it. It's finished. But it's never quite finished. [*Laughs*]

In your relation to performers, how do you frame their work? How do you ensure that each individual is still there and not put into a form?

This is always my fear. But it's important to know that while we are working, I am always waiting. I am trying not to force the material and say, 'I think you should do this or that.' I am always waiting for something to come and to understand what's coming. And then maybe suggest something. How to do this material, this person, and develop a story, or a scene or an action or whatever. Then this material becomes a little bit mine, too. We are starting to share the idea. And by this sharing, I might understand what kind of motivations are behind this material. Because it's not mine. It's performance material.

I know that this material cannot be performed in empty space. It's always put into something. And I am trying to give this material a kind of – let's say concept. Sometimes it is a concept, because I build my own little story up around it. But what is more important, I am always trying to read this material through the relationship – because the relationship between the performer and the spectator is the most important relationship we are building, and it's the most important focus for what we are doing. I am trying to find structures or frames that will amplify the performer, to support him.

Often I have noticed how important it is just to find the borders of the scenes. Where should the scene start? We started yesterday's performance [*Casablanca Therapy*] completely differently than before. In Marie-Louise [Stentebjerg]'s scene, she is a victim and this sets the tone for the whole performance. And when I was thinking about it, I said to myself, 'Yes, my god, that's why we called it *Therapy*!' So after seven or eight performances I understand something of what we are doing. You simply need a lot of time to recognize what you are doing. And this is often connected with the capability to push yourself to a distance of your work. Then you will see.

What seems to be common to all your performances is the vulnerability of your performers. Why is that always there?

There is one important decision about our work: We are always trying to find a way to step down from the stage. To be on an equal relationship, to feel community with the audience. The stage is always a kind of power position. We are the selected ones to be there. So we have to find what we call a strategy of humiliating ourselves somehow. We have to find a way of being human on stage and not being performers or actors. We know that we are, but still we need these steps down.

It's a decision, and the lack of scenography and costumes is also a decision. It's one of our rules of reduction, and it's also connected with the name *Via Negativa*. Let's avoid everything that we don't need. Push it away. Usually I am really radical about it. 'This is just static shit, put it away, you don't need it. What you have to say, simply say it.' Then often we see that real stuff starts to come out. When you reduce everything to the bare presence. Empty stage. 'Here, there are people. Let's do it now.' We push ourselves into a really hard position.

Does all your work take place in a rehearsal hall?

No, we also sit around a table and talk a lot. I like to meet with the performers to have a drink or a coffee and discuss the idea. Because my belief is that it's better not to rehearse if it's not clear what we are rehearsing. It's better to discuss it and then try. But this is a later stage in our work. In the beginning I'm just pushing them to just go, do, show, show, show something, until we can all see that it's going nowhere anymore. We also discuss through emails if the performance is not in Ljubljana. They send me their ideas if they have something new. I give my solutions or ideas. Then maybe they reply, 'I don't understand you. Now I am stuck.' So I say, 'Okay, forget about it. Send me something new.' I like to make this constant pressure on people. They are responsible. If they want to have a show, they have to do something for it. And then I try to assure them that if they are giving the best of themselves, then the show will be good, because I take the responsibility of packing it in a way so that it will work.

Last year, I did a performance with a dance group from Ljubljana. They called me and said, 'Bojan, you make such interesting performances, we would like to work with you. We would like to test your way of working.' And I was happy. My God: five dancers! A completely different logic. They usually have a more abstract thinking and I am really concrete. For the theme, I proposed to them: 'If I tell you to do the best of you, what will you do on stage? Think about what this could be. The best of you.' The deal was that if you give the best of you, then there is no chance that the performance won't be a success. Everybody agreed that it made sense. And everybody tried to work on the subject *the best of me*. What is that?

They tried this and that, and this and that, also beyond dance. Immediately from the beginning they decided that it was not about the dance, it was about human qualities. They tried to find stories about this, but they were not satisfied with what they found. Then, after months of working they realized that actually, we don't know what is the best, we can only think of what other people think is the best about us. Our mothers, for instance. Why can't we decide what is the best of each of us? Maybe we don't know, maybe we are afraid to define it, or maybe – and this was somehow the final realization – we are not satisfied with anything. We cannot decide if this or this or this is the best, because it's not. Nobody was satisfied.

I liked this conclusion a lot. And then I decided to do the show in a negative way and to call it *Cut Out* [2009, production by EN-KNAP], and we just showed the small pieces that we decided were not good enough to be in the show. The whole performance is 'cut outs' of the performance. It was a really simple show, and I liked it a lot. Again this logic reached the point where we had nothing, but still you always have a lot! You just have to recognize it somehow, and this is the hardest part of what we are doing. In art and also in general. To recognize what is good, what has worth. I find this the hardest.

How do audiences react to your performances?

Very often it happens that the audience is shocked by our performances. It is not our intention to shock people. We are trying to avoid it. But we know that if, for instance, there is a radical body action on stage – as there often is in our performances – that will shock people. But I don't like shock, because shock is something that closes your perception. And then you start to defend yourself. That's why we also use a lot of humour, because this is the door that opens people somehow. If we are on the track of something that we know will be shocking, we are always trying to find the next step in the story that will somehow invite people back into it. I call it crawling behind their backs. Maybe in the beginning there is a ... *bam!* [*slaps his hands together*], and then we sneak around and tell them that it is not so hard or so negative after all.

This is really important to us, because shocking people is not difficult, but on the other hand to avoid something because you don't want to be hard on the audience is also not good. You have to do what you have to do. But you have to really think about the strategy for doing it. I'm not talking about dramaturgy, but about strategy because it is relation and communication. And to have a good strategy means that you know what you will produce with this move, and if you know that, then you can probably find the next move that will correct it or support it or destroy it, or show people that this was just a joke or that you were just playing with their expectations and so on.

The essential

And for your specific process, what is, do you think, the essential condition for it to be successful?

Well, for me, it's time. And the space, of course. But no, you can rehearse, I don't know – in the park, if you don't have a rehearsal room, but it's time, it's time. To be able to take as much time as you would like to. That is the most important for me. I don't like time pressure. I know that we need a frame. But our frame will often be that we know we will do this performance in the autumn, maybe in September or October or November. We know we have to do it this year. And we usually start in the beginning of the year. So we have this whole year of slowly working and thinking and asking questions, because that is also one of my basic tools. Constantly asking the question why, and looking for an interesting focus for what we are doing. So to me it's time; time is precious. And what I like about the theatre is that we can steal time. Often I have this feeling that we have to steal this time for us. And I like it a lot when we are in the moments of not knowing what to do. To me these are the most creative moments. Until I know what we are doing I am not satisfied, because I think, 'Yes, yes, yes, yes…' And then we approach this question that nobody knows anymore. *Then* it is time to work. And that is the most difficult. I like to afford – I think we should always afford to be in the position of not knowing. For me that is the most precious moment. And a lot of people get really frustrated about that situation. 'I don't know what to do.' Well, *now* do something. Now something might come.

Problems

And what do you think is the biggest problem or difficulty that always comes up?

Again, it's about time for me. Yes, it's time. Because when time pressure is pushing you to force the decisions about the work, then you are doing harm to the work. Decisions are best when they jump out of the work by themselves and you just have to recognize them. When you are forcing the work, in my opinion you make lots of mistakes. And that is the worst you can do to your work. But usually time means money, and everything is connected. The money, the contract and everything.

Dreams

So what would you like to change about the process? Or try out? If anything is possible, anything would succeed?

I'm interested in finding out if it's possible to develop a new performance out of a small piece of a performance that you have already done. Then you build this new performance and the next performance out of a small piece of this performance. And so on. That's what we are trying to do now. That's why our new project is called *Via Nova* instead of *Via Negativa*. We just took a small piece from one performance and said, 'Okay, this is interesting.' While we were doing the show we knew that we didn't have enough time to do this interesting thing, because we needed to do a whole show about it. So afterwards we said, 'Let's take this and go for it.' Now may be the time to do it.

That was one wish of mine that I am now trying to realize. And I don't have enough time to think about a new wish because I am in the middle of trying to do something with this one. But I also wish for the project [*Via Negativa*] to grow and grow. That's why I call it a project, not a group or company. Because I want to bring new people into it. To give them the experiences we have. Because it's a simple tool for creating theatre and developing this work. And maybe now we can do it a bit faster than while we were learning how to do it. That is also a wish: each year to have an opportunity to do *Via Negativa*, do it with completely new people from different fields of work – dancers, musicians, visual artists. But you have to have time for this, and money, opportunity and so on.

Lately, I have been doing more than one performance at a time, because I am doing small-scale performances now. Solo performances or duets, for instance. And to give people more time to think I am jumping from one piece to another and it helps me to have a distance. To not be completely in one piece. Just jump into one, and be completely in it for a week or two, and then jump out and be with another. When you return to the first one, you see something new because you are doing two or three of them separately.

Something different, something new, something that helps you in the work you are doing concurrently. That is really helpful for me. So I like to be busy with several things. Also, because I cannot make a living from doing theatre, I work for a marketing agency in Ljubljana as a copy-writer. So I write commercials. I like it because I can leave the theatre for half an hour just to make stupid jokes and slogans for radio and television. I like the tasks because I hate them. It is really a love-hate-situation, because they are impossible. For instance, I got this task: 'We need a new name for milk.' A milk product. And I think, 'My God, it's just milk.' 'Yes, yes, but we would like to have a brand.' Okay, so they want an identity, character. But it's milk. So I decided that the name would be Mu. And everybody thought that I was making a joke. But I persisted with this name, 'It's a good name, it's two letters: Mu. It's simple, for design it's great. It's international. Everybody will know. What do cows do? Moo. I think it's a great idea.'

And they sold this idea to the company. So now we have this brand called Mu, and it's great. But then what happened? They wanted a commercial campaign for the product. And of course, for these commercials I got the idea that the cows should discuss how important they are in the lives of humans. I really liked the idea. But they couldn't sell it because the company told them that they didn't want to do anything with cows. 'My God, you're making milk! And we called the product Mu!' 'No, we don't want the commercial to have anything to do with cows.' And I couldn't crack this problem. I was really angry with milk. [*Laughs*] I started thinking about parrots, but no, no… And in the end, another company did it.

I like these distractions in my work. A lot of different problems. The biggest problem is if I don't have a problem, because then I don't know what to do.[1]

Interview: Barbara Simonsen

Bojan Jablanovec (SI)
Bojan Jablanovec (born 1961) is a Slovenian director dedicated to theatre research. He is interested in theatre as a medium of communication rather than as aesthetics. Using reduction as a working method, he focuses on the relationship between the performer and the audience and on the question of the real in this relationship. In 2002, he founded *Via Negativa*, an international contemporary performing arts project.

Select works
Seven Deadly Sins (2002–2008)
Via Nova (2009–2011)
Via New Territories (2011)
VN Lab/ Laboratory for contemporary performing arts (since 2012)

Website
www.vntheatre.com

Note

1 This interview was made before a live audience at Entré Scenen, Aarhus, Denmark, as part of the programme of the East Gate Europe Festival 2010. Some of the questions in the interview were posed by the audience.

12

Elizabeth LeCompte

Why

Why did you choose theatre, or how did you end up in theatre?

Well, I went to school in art – art history and painting/drawing… Oh boy, this is really tough, because there is a lot of strands of how it happened. But the most salient one, I would say, is that when I was in school I started working on the weekends at a café, and the café decided to have a theatre company. I was a waitress there during the weekends, and the woman who ran the café went down to New York and hired a bunch of actors to come up and live communally in an old Victorian house that she had in this town called Saratoga Springs.[1] And as the theatre side of the operation developed alongside of the café, which was for folk singing, basically, they needed people to help out. She hired a man, a wonderful Welshman, to take over the theatre. His name was John Wynne-Evans; he was gay and he hired all these very handsome, fabulous men and no women. So whenever they needed somebody I was forced to go in. I was just terrible. But I loved the world of it, and I started running the lights and doing that kind of thing. And I met a man there named Spalding Gray, and we both just… I didn't want to go on with painting, it was during the time when minimalism was happening, and I was disconnected from it. I was very connected with the political and social situation at the time, in the late sixties. And somehow I think got dragged into it because… I didn't know how I was going to make a living as an artist. And I was offered a job right away through Spalding's connections to assist and direct for Richard Schechner's company The Performance Group, and it paid so much more money than I could make selling postcards.

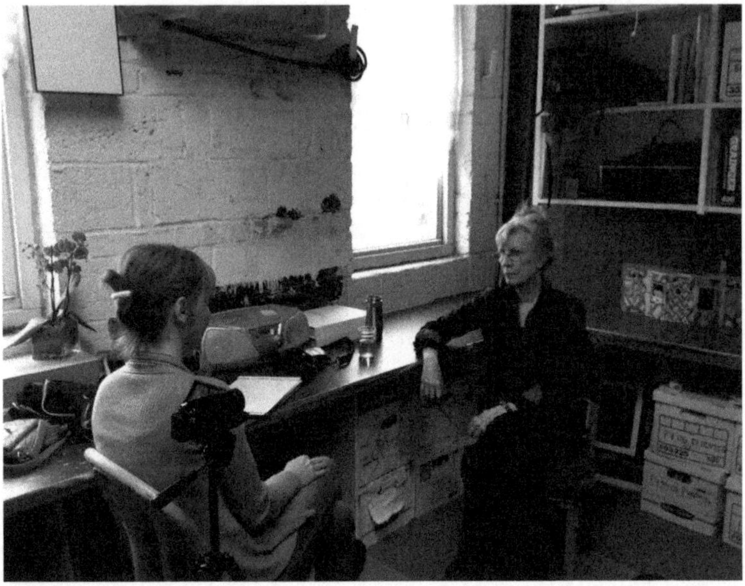

Figure 3 Barbara Simonsen and Elizabeth LeCompte, New York, March 2016

Even though I graduated from college with a double major of art history and painting I didn't go on to graduate school, because I didn't know how I was going to make a living. At that time the thought for me, coming from New Jersey, a middle-class household, I didn't see a way of doing it. So I think I kind of veered off. I joined this company as an assistant director, and I was also the photographer and I helped with the sets. So it was like everything, because I liked the social world, I liked the politics involved, and I mean politics in the biggest sense of the word. And I liked texts as well as the visual world. So I just slipped in very easily and became almost immediately a director. That's one strand.

I think it's the first time I've heard someone say that they chose theatre because it was the more secure job!

Yes, but you have to realize that when I was coming up, I couldn't… I graduated very well placed in my class, and I couldn't get a job as an assistant or associate curator at any museum, but the men that graduated in the next college went right to curating. I went right to selling postcards. It was another time. I started a bookstore first, with my sister and another artist that I knew – he still works with us as a filmmaker – and the bookstore couldn't make any money either. So the three of us had to separate out and I decided to come back to New York, and the two of them went on with the bookstore, because it couldn't support three people. And that's when I was offered a job at the theatre that paid, amazing, seventy dollars a week. It was just amazing at the time. It's gone down since then [*laughs*]. Well, almost, in terms of what the dollar is worth. But that's why. And in those days it was just another world. And you could live on very little. We bought this place [The Performing Garage, 33 Wooster St, NY] for almost nothing, way back in 1972. I can't even tell you, it's worth two thousand times as much as we bought it for.

How

Can you describe a typical rehearsal process for you, as concretely as possible?

They feel so different to me, but probably they're not. The rehearsal process is always dependent on the material that we start to work with. Sometimes it's a play, sometimes it's just an idea. It's always some kind of a text, but it can be a play or just documentary material, or it can be writing of some other kind. So if it's a play it's very simple. I never read it before I go into rehearsal. I decide on it, either because somebody wants to do it in the company, or someone's told me we should do it, because it would be right for us or we could get money for it. Something like that. Or I've heard about it or I read it when I was very young. Then I get together with the company and we read it. Or whoever we get to come.

But then you've already decided to do it?

No, no. We'll read it, and then sometimes I'll go, 'Oh, that's interesting' – and I don't go back and read it on my own. I get another bunch of people maybe together, or a smaller cast, or we read it again – the same people. By that time I'll have a vision of how to stage it. That comes first. I'll have some idea of the style, how I want to hear it, or how I don't want to hear it. Sometimes it's just the negative. I want to find some new way of hearing it that I don't even know about. And then we start, if it's a play, by trying to stage it. But I have usually two or maybe sometimes three ideas in mind at the same time, and they don't … what's the word I'm looking for…? They don't augment each other or illuminate each other. They are two totally separate ideas. Like for one play, *Phèdre* [*To You, The Birdie (Phèdre)*, 2001], I had an idea: I was really interested in thirties and fifties architecture in America, mainly in the West Coast. Just for structure. So I wanted to make the space into that structure and then fit the script into that. How would people move in that space? And I wasn't thinking, 'Oh, this is the right text for that, or, it's not the right text.' I don't even think about that right away. And then I had a third thing for that text that was… I had so much work to do with that text, I had to figure out what the voice of the text was, that I needed time to think and just watch people on stage. So if I do that, I just invent a game or a structure or something, usually some kind of a sport. For that one it was ping-pong, which became badminton – so that I can watch them and put music to it, just doing something on the stage while I can think. Because I get so nervous when they have to just stare at me and I don't have anything. That's usually there for just about every piece. There is something that I give them to do so I can watch them in the space. It doesn't have to be a game, it's not a game so much as a series of actions that they have to do, that have nothing to do with the text, usually. At the end they join into the text in a nice way – if we work long enough, it works itself together.

And then I have this other area of sound that I'm always interested in. I'm interested in some kind of music and sometimes it comes from the text, but usually it doesn't. Usually it's something I'm interested in. Like for this last piece, the Pinter [*The Room*, 2016], I was really interested in this Chinese music, because we had just been to China. So that was over here. And then the physical structure was from a

Chinese comedy form called crosstalk, how they had to imitate or simulate that structure on the stage. And then the text. And so I work those three things, and I think a lot of that's just intuition. It's not as if I go… [*waves in all directions*], but it's things that are interesting to me and they seem to come together because I have the space and the time. It's a real luxury. The only thing I don't have is money, but I have plenty of time and space.

How much time will a rehearsal process usually take?

Well, in the old days I would be working on one piece and depending on whether it was a script… A script is much easier, but if I'm having to make the script and do all the other things at the same time, with the company – we always collaborate terrifically on that whoever is in the room – it could take me anywhere from two months, two and a half months, to two years. Something like *Cry, Trojans!* [2014] took three years because of many, many things that were a problem. And *L.S.D. (…Just the high points…)*, something I did back in the eighties [1984], took me two years. But it's not steady. Because we have this place we're always doing in rep one of our other pieces, or touring those pieces, so there are these big gaps in the middle. So we'll work no more than two months at a time, maybe two and a half months, then I'll take off, do an older piece and then come back to it. That's the two years. Altogether it's not more than six months, or even four months.

So after that first phase where you give them an activity and let your ideas come, what does it go into after that?

Yeah, I don't want to say 'give them an activity', because I don't really give them, it just comes up, we figure out something to do. I like to feel the room and figure out what I want to see somehow. And they'll usually come up with an answer for it.

Then I start to place and combine in the space. I only hear and see in three dimensions, so I can't really hear something flat. I have to hear it in the space and I get them on their feet almost immediately. We don't do any analysis of the text in the traditional way. We do talk about it and we'll read stuff, like today we're working on something that is a feminist panel from the early 1970s and we spent a good deal of time reading this Baudrillard-thing. It's just because I found it over there when I was going through some of my things to throw away. And it links up, but it will never be in the piece. There's a lot of that time. Because we have that kind of time, people bring things in, we talk about politics… We usually talk about what's happening before we start, I don't know why, we're just social. Everybody's pretty social. And then that all feeds into the work. But pretty organically. The big thing for me is that I don't have a system. I probably do, but I don't want to know what it is. Because I go in and I don't know what the script's about and I wasn't in theatre so much that the things people bring me… I have no idea. I've heard about the play, and I have to figure out what it is for me. I don't see theatre as a literary art; it is a collaboration between the director, the performers and the writer. How you balance that is extremely important to me. All three things are extremely important, but it is not a literary activity, it's an event.

How do you move from trying things out to deciding where it's going to land?

That again depends. Sometimes if someone has brought me a piece that they want to do I'll follow them. With Spalding, I just followed him. He would say, 'I want to do this,' and I would go, 'Oh, what would you like to do?' Then I work with that, edit it, stage it – find out what he wants to do, because if you can find out what someone really wants to do, you've got gold [*smiles*]. I look for that in all the performers. To try to find that out and then somehow push it toward what I want to see. In that there is this kind of dialectic… Sometimes it's a struggle, but struggle is always good, because we each give something. When it works. When it doesn't work it's horrendous and I go away crying, but when it works it's pretty easy. I'd say 50 per cent of the time it doesn't work and 50 per cent it does. And then I mix and match, because I'm a good editor. I'm not a great editor, but I'm a good editor. Someone like Scott Shepherd, who is working with us, is a terrific editor – and so they help me with scripts, because you know, I can almost attach anything to any part of the script. Just like I can attach any part of the music, I'm very… What's the word? Catholic, I guess. My tastes range – and I don't use music or movement to illustrate. There's always at least three different systems that are going on at the same time, so I have to mix and match, find out what brings out – at this point it's the dance, at this point… How can I always hear it, and at the same time how can I make it so that that part of the hearing it is made bigger by the other part, not obscured. That's hard, because we're such a literary culture. It's hard to do, and I have to take some risks sometimes of making it not as easy as it is, say, in a normal theatre production. Because I hear sound as well as words.

Do you work that into the script, practically? Do you have a script with text or do you have all these layers in there like a score?

It depends. If I'm working like I'm working on this piece, it's these layers. Every day there is a new script with things next to it. But when I'm working like with the Pinter (play) I just follow every stage direction, I follow everything as closely as possible and I try to get in, why it was in his or her head. I don't think of it that way, but I see that that's what I'm doing. Trying to figure out why he would say sit down there, how do I get that person to sit down there, because I have no seat. Do I bring a chair in? Do I say sitting down is something else? It's always making translations and ways of bringing the script to us or to me, as well as going to the script. That's the fun of it for me. And when I've gone too far and I've lost the writer, when I've gone too far and I've lost myself – it's that play.

Do you continue rehearsing and adjusting after the opening?

Oh yes. All the time. Because we have to open the things before they're really finished, and I love having the audience come in because they tell me everything. Mostly they tell me about myself, because if I don't want to watch it while they are watching it I know it's not me. So then I have to go back in there and find out when I will feel totally comfortable no matter what it is, no matter if they hate it or love it, I'm safe. And that's hard to get to. If people love something [*applauding*] and I'm embarrassed and don't, it's not me, I'm caught in this terrible place, where I want to go with them, but I can't bear to watch it unless I go with me.

The essential

In your experience, what is the essential condition for a rehearsal process to succeed or go well?

A company of people who are committing themselves to that project for that moment. Totally committing. They don't have to trust me. I've worked with many people who didn't trust me, but went along for other reasons. It's great, no problem. As long as we can come to something. But I have to be able to work with the sound, the video, the lighting and the performers all at the same time, because to make the pieces I don't make them separately. The technical people are working in the same way as the performers. So when we make something we try to make the whole mix. Usually I think what happens is a score is added on later. For me, I make the sound score with the sound guys at the same time as I am making the oral score. I need that. They have to be there in the space.

How does one pick the right people? Or when do you know that the people are right?

I don't pick them! [*Laughs.*] And I don't ever know that they're right. I just know that they are there. They have made a commitment to be there. That's all. Because if I got everybody that was right, I can't imagine that, I mean, theatre is about conflict. And I depend on that, I depend on people being in the space who are going to say, 'I can't do that,' or 'I don't know that,' or 'You're wrong.' I depend on that, because it forces me to not go back on myself, I would be so bored. I mean, I've made maybe sixty pieces, and I would have been so bored by the tenth piece that I would have… I would have done what what's-his-name did… I would have quit theatre. What keeps me going is that I never know who is going to say no, and then I'm going to have to deal with it. I was just thinking of that now, I'm always having that and it's very exciting. It's also frustrating. But very exciting in the end.

They pick me. I pick them by committing the time. But people come. Sometimes we need someone that we don't have, after we've read and read, maybe four times we've read it with people, and I think, 'I'm not hearing this voice.' It's like music. I don't have the right instrument. And then we go looking for a friend. Whoever's available. Katie [Valk] and I and usually now Ari [Fliakos] are the people who are at the core. The core changes over the years, but now the core is Ari and Scott [Shepherd] and Katie and myself and Enver [Chakartash] and a couple of other people on the tech. We'll get together and say, 'What about this person?' It's a really wide range of people that we know now. And then it's somebody who can commit to the project, because everybody has so much to do and nobody has enough money. So it really works kind of naturally.

A lot of people come in by interning. Katie was an intern when she was twenty-one. Ari was an intern when he was twenty-two. Scott didn't come as an intern, but I saw him in a piece by one of my interns who went off and made his own company. I saw Scott in that and brought him into this company as well, so he is in both companies. That kind of thing. It's not a family – well, maybe it is, because we don't all get along, and we don't really all socialize very much. But when we come together it's very clear, we're there for the duration, and you have your choice. You can sit back and not give anything, and I'll find some place depending who you are, or you can come forward and say, 'I need this,' and we work it out. The only thing that's hard for me is if people feel uncomfortable with that kind of collaboration. If they are not willing to give up something personal in the collaboration. That's a problem, because I'm looking for what they are going to give that they love about themselves, and some people aren't able to do that. Especially I think it's hard for people who want to work alone as solo people, so I don't work so long with those people, because they find their own thing and go off.

Problems

And in your experience, what is then the biggest problem in a rehearsal process? Something that always comes up or can never be solved?

Losing someone. I lose people all the time. It comes up all the time, and it's always a problem. That I've 'trained' somebody – quote, unquote, because I don't really train someone – we find some kind of way of working together that's fantastic, it's working great – and they want to go on and make their own work. Or they want to go into films, or… I never say you have to stay, I would never, I never make any contracts with anybody, they can go any time they want. But that's always a readjustment to a new person coming in. But in the end I think it's what's kept me alive. Because they come in with new material so that I have to rethink everything and find what they are. And that changes the work. It changes me. It's hard, but it's not fatal.

Money is fatal. That's very difficult. That's always the problem. But, somebody would say, 'What are you complaining about?' We might not have money, but we have a lot of other things.

Dreams

If you could change or try out anything in the rehearsal process, what would you want to do?

[*Considers, shakes her head.*] Nothing. No, I can't think of anything.

Do you think it's because you are in fact able to change things every time? Or is it that you feel you've found the…?

No, I never feel I've found anything. I'm always like on the brink of some kind of failure. I don't know why I say that, I think I say it because I can't think of anything I want, except a little more money, not a lot. The hardest thing for me is working this long, and in the States here it's not a value. Our longevity, and what we do, is not valued the way it is, say, in Europe. So it's harder and harder for me to get money as I get older. Sometimes I think, 'Why didn't I stay in Europe?' But I couldn't, because I'm so politically... Everything that I do is about this world, so I would have gone into a very different kind of much more using my art without words in the same way. The texts wouldn't have been the same.

No, the only thing is really that problem here in the States about the value of women, of older women. It's very difficult here. And the value of staying in the small venues. If I had gone on and was making pieces big enough for BAM [Brooklyn Academy of Music]... I don't go to BAM because I don't want to make pieces on a big stage. I like the size of the stage. I don't like any audience bigger than 350 people. Maybe tops 400 depending on the piece. Because we're in the same room, and for me it's about that relationship and I don't want to lose that. And I sit in the audience every night so I certainly don't want to lose it. I want to feel that connection. But that's not what's rewarded here. It's difficult to convince people that we're still influential even though we're still playing to a smaller house. But it's a small complaint. The fact that I'm here and we're still working...

What I recognize is that if you choose to work in small venues and do experimental projects and always try new things people assume that when you 'grow up' you want to go somewhere else...

Yes, exactly.

But some of us don't.

Some of us don't. Exactly.

Interview: Barbara Simonsen

Elizabeth LeCompte (US)
Elizabeth LeCompte (born 1944) is a director of theatre, dance and media. She is a founding member of The Wooster Group, a performance group based in New York at The Performing Garage since 1975, whose work LeCompte is still directing. The Wooster Group has celebrated numerous successes in America and internationally.

Select works
North Atlantic (1984, 1999, 2010)
House/Lights (1998, 2005)
Hamlet (2007, 2012)
The Room (2016)

Website
www.thewoostergroup.org

Note

1 Caffè Lena, founded in 1960 by Bill and Lena Spencer.

13

Richard Lowdon

Why

How did you end up in theatre?

I did a course in Exeter University, which was English and Drama. The course was very practical. You would work with a small group of people, like ten people, for three years and you'd make things constantly. It wasn't actor's training or anything like that. Every five weeks you would do a project on somebody, maybe a project on Brecht, and the thing that you would do in the end was not a Brecht play, but something in response to that in some way. I suppose in a way for us it was a case of making things together as a group, and that was the only way we really understood how to make theatre. That you just went in to a room with a group of people and talked about things and then you would try things on your feet as much as possible. At the university was where most of the company met. Most of us were studying the same thing, spread across three different years.

In that small group of people, you would do everything together. I think at the end of your second year you were given like a little bit of text, and everybody had to be in six other people's things. And then at the end of your final year you directed a little project. So it was intense and practical. It was really great.

The aesthetic of the course was very much like in the sixties – that was the only problem that we had with it. As a group, we started making work outside of the course that was a little bit more in response to the things that we were seeing, and we were working with a slightly different aesthetic. So by the time we left university we had decided that we were going to form a theatre company. Because we'd seen people

Figure 4 Richard Lowdon, Barbara Simonsen and Isabelle Reynaud, Aarhus, June 2008

who really impressed us, and we wanted to be like them! We spent the first two years copying other people's work and sort of trying to emulate.

I think I chose that course because it was the most interesting. I was about nineteen, and the places that I applied to were very interested either in text or directing, and there just seemed to be something much more exiting about this. Also, because part of the selection process was that you went for a weekend and so it wasn't like going for an interview. It was a whole weekend with a group of people and you really felt part of something. And then they were very good at writing letters saying, 'We think you're really great, please please come.' Of course, flattery really works. [*Laughs*]

Did you know you wanted to act?

Well, I'd been involved in some amateur things when I was young. But actually, when I left school I wanted to become a saddle maker, and I did an apprenticeship for about six months and then decided I really didn't like it. So I went a slightly strange path. I was thinking more and more about theatre, and I had a brother who was ten years older than me and who was very interested in theatre, and I remember him giving me *The Empty Space* by Peter Brook. Which at that age, when I read it, it so much chimed for me, about the dead theatre and all of that, and I thought, actually, theatre could be something quite exciting. So I spent a lot of time at fifteen or sixteen going to the theatre. Sort of enjoying it, but actually being quite bored and not really allowing myself to say that I was bored. So that was exciting, maybe I could go and do this course. Also, I suppose I was drawn to it because it wasn't necessarily about acting or directing. It was about making theatre and people who came out of that course would go into a number of different things. It was never really for sure that you would end up in theatre even if you did that course.

And I guess I was lucky, really, because we managed to get together with a group of people who shared the same tastes. That's just luck.

How

And so you have been working in that group ever since?

Yeah, not exactly the same group as at university, but basically that's how we've worked. The core company is six people. Five of them are from the Exeter course. When we started there were seven of us, and two people left after the first two years. And then Claire [Marshall], who has been part of the company since 1989, joined, and she came from a slightly different background.

Can you talk about working in an ensemble like that compared to short-term projects?

It's hard, because in a way that's the only thing I've ever done. It never occurred to us to do anybody else's text, for instance. Because all we knew was that you went into a room with a group of people and then you made something.

I suppose you start making a process that's quite idiosyncratic. It's not like there is any kind of methodology to it. It's just very much born out of the people that we are. Initially we used to certainly try not to spend too much time talking. We still say that, but actually we can spend like a week talking and never get on our feet. We're terrible, in a way. I think maybe it's as you've made more and more things, you're able to project in your mind the model of a show from the merest scrap of improvisation. You say, 'Ah, well, this is kind of interesting ten minutes – very likely, the show would follow this, this and this.' And in a way you create these little models, or you say, 'Yeah, that's a nice idea for ten minutes, but it's not really a show, so let's just put that over there.'

Do you tend to think about the same models or are they all each individual's models?

People do have differences and are obviously drawn more towards certain things than others. But that sort of modelling process we tend do together. We tend to do everything pretty much about consensus. If you really believe something, you have to eventually win everybody over to your point of view. But I think the important thing is that – in terms of processes – we're not very precious about our ideas. So we're very easy to say okay, if we try something and it doesn't work, let's leave it. And I suppose in a process where you are working together for so long, quite often you come back to things. So something that was maybe in a rehearsal process for one show, an idea that never made it into the show, suddenly comes back three years later, or four years later, and you say, 'Oh, do you remember the thing that we did with the… the gorilla? That might be interesting. Have you got that in the cupboard? Let's get that out.' In a way, you're following a lot of different strands.

Perhaps in that sense it's easier having worked together for a long time, and in the beginning deciding that we were going to work together for a long time. Because it meant that the first show was not necessarily *the* most important one. I think for young companies, very often you want to put everything into the first show. For us, it was like, okay, this is the first thing that we are making, and then we'll make this, and then we'll see what happens when we make that. And after five years you have this sense of, 'Well, this show is the thing that we make next.' And inevitably, everything is flawed in some way, and you can look at it and go, 'Well, I don't know, that doesn't really work' – but at a certain point, you have to stop changing things and then make the next thing. I think that was a lesson that we learned quite early on and that probably helped us.

That's what you can do with an ensemble. You can go back three years and say, 'Do you remember that idea?' and everybody remembers it. You can't do that in projects.

Exactly. We were talking about this the other day, saying that in a way that's a virtue, but it can be a trap as well. Because you're constantly comparing it back to models of things you've made previously saying, 'Ah yes, well, of course in this show it works like this, and in that show it works like that.'

I always think this is interesting that when you've improvised you have a bunch of material on the table, and you're trying to structure it, or organize it. Quite often, what you end up doing is applying a kind of thinking that you have from before, to that material. Then often we start to say, 'You know what, maybe we're asking the wrong questions of what this is.' That I think is the hardest thing: to ask the right questions of the material that you've made, so you follow where *it* wants to take you, rather than were you want to push it. We often talk about what the show wants to do rather than what we want to do with the show.

It's like when you get on your feet and make something, and for days and days you haven't made anything very interesting, and then one day you make like ten minutes and you go, 'Ah. Don't know what that is… Why is that interesting?' And then you spend a week just doing that again and again, thinking maybe having done that, you'll roll off the end of it into something else. But you never get any further although it's still interesting because you're trying to push things in a certain direction. And the sort of happiest bits of creation, I think, are when you don't feel like you're pushing it. It goes somewhere and you have to follow what that is.

I suppose that's tied in a way to the fact that when we're working on shows we don't tend to start from a theme or really have any fixed starting points. We just start from things that interest us in one way or another – be it a costume or a piece of music or a mood. It could be anything.

The essential

What do you think is the most essential set-up or condition to make that process work?

It's really difficult to say. Having your own rehearsal space – we're not in that position at the moment – but for years that was very important to us. That we had a room that was permanently ours, that we could go into twenty-four hours a day. It was hugely important. Then you could try anything whenever it came to you. Also, we joke about this a lot, having a cupboard next to your rehearsal room that is full of stuff that you've used in other shows or things you've collected. So that when you're stuck you can go into the cupboard and get something. I mean, they are stupid things, but important. Increasingly, I think daylight might be quite important! [*Laughs.*] Because we work all the time in a black box and it's good because you can light things as you are making them, so you're working with all of those elements at the same time, but sometimes you really want to be able to open the windows and let some light in.

And a lot of coffee… I don't know. It's an interesting question, because it's very difficult to answer. It's really hard to figure out what's essential. When we make a piece, quite often we spend the last two weeks in a theatre, which I think has been really important to us. And generally somewhere that's not even in England, so everybody is really away for two weeks. You don't have any of your normal responsibilities, children and so on, and so you can really just focus. Those intensive periods of time are very important, I think.

And the people, of course. We know we have to have the right people, but what makes them the right people?

I suppose sharing the same kind of taste is pretty essential. Not necessarily even in theatre. I think we all came together as a group because we liked the same music and the same films more than we liked theatre. In fact, when we started we didn't really like theatre at all. I imagine that if it had been easier to get hold of cameras in those days, we would have all become filmmakers rather than theatre-makers. But sharing things with those people is very important. Both the similarity and the difference are important. I suppose I don't think about the people very much because we have worked in a group for so long, so it's like making something with your family. I take that for granted.

But when we work with other people, or when we bring other people in for projects, we tend to not do that on a one off basis. We'll work with some people in a collaborative way over a number of years. And the fact that they're from different backgrounds is useful. On *Bloody Mess* [2004] we worked with Wendy Houstoun who did the set, and Davis Freeman who comes out of a more European physical dance theatre background. Bruno Roubicek, who's been in straight theatre, but trained at Jacques Lecoq. What was interesting about all of that was that you had all this fusion of languages to talk about what you are doing. Wendy would always talk in terms of the kind of energy that was flowing through different sections, and Bruno was very interested in the character, and how the character worked. Things we never talk about, but it's interesting to hit against those things. When you're in a group of people, you tend to assume certain roles and positions within that group, and when you change the number of people or add more people, of course the dynamics change and then everything has to readjust, realign. That's hugely important.

What do you think the relationship is between the space and what's actually created? Do you think that different rehearsal spaces influence the way you make theatre? Topics you choose, the way you work?

I think it's hard to separate that out from your own personal history and the whole economic and political climate at the times that you were making things. When we were first rehearsing in Sheffield, the place we were rehearsing was a classically abandoned sort of industrial space. But at that time, Sheffield was a very, very poor post-industrial city, and I think in a way a lot of our work was made in response to that environment. These days perhaps that's less true. But I do think that the dungeon that we've been working in recently is probably not good for our health!

Perhaps the biggest change was going and actually working in theatres. Rehearsing in theatres, because then you can actually sit back, and the ability to sit fifty meters away from something that you are making I think is hugely important. If you could have your absolute wish list you'd have a theatre for eight weeks in which you could make the piece, and then you really live in it and it feels like yours and you understand exactly what you are doing with it. You always encounter problems of transposing something that you've made in a room, where you've been very much on top of it, and then you put it into the theatre for the first time, and you sit back and the thing that seemed wonderfully exciting and made your eye go like this [*looks from side to side*] – once you sit twenty metres back you look at it and go, 'Hm… Great…'

Problems

What are the worst problems of the rehearsal process, or problems that always come up?

Getting stuck, I think. That's probably our worst problem. Getting stuck is when you have an idea, and you like it, and it doesn't deliver you very much, and you can't seem to put anything else with it. It seems to resist anything else being with it. You can't follow it either. It's that classic thing of having ten minutes of material that you really love, that you hope will be the key to the show – and actually doesn't turn out to be the key at all. And you feel like you hammer at it and hammer at it, trying to lead it in different directions, and you hit a blank. And you're in a position of saying, 'Okay, we need to just start somewhere else.'

And the 'we need to start somewhere else' is always really hard because you find yourself pulled back to the thing you were doing. To put that in context, quite often what we hope is that when we come into the rehearsal room at the beginning of the process, we will have a number of different ideas or half ideas. Generally, nothing fully formed, but some half-baked ideas that can go on the table, and we can play with this and if that doesn't go anywhere we'll play with this. The worst situation is when you come in and really all you have is one thing, and you play with it and you go, 'Hmm… Anything else? No. Then let's play with this again.' That's really difficult.

And the 'getting stuck-ness' is something that I think we experience on every single thing we make, at a certain point. We used to joke that the way to get out of it was that by Friday afternoon, you'd be so frustrated with it that you would do anything, and in this sort of Friday afternoon craziness you'd end up doing something that would somehow un-stick you, and finally you would feel like there was somewhere else to go. So I think that's a problem, but I have no idea how to solve it. That's the bizarre thing.

The process we've just been through and the show we've just made have been particularly difficult, because we'd set out to make a show with five people in it, and all the things that we were making would start off with improvisations with a couple of people. Thinking we would start with two, and then probably we could add more people in. But we were making these things that very quickly sealed themselves into something that really worked with two people. Then you felt, oh, that's nice, but why would you put anybody else with that? That's lovely.

Maybe that's a show in itself but then you put that to the side. In a way, our whole process was making things that really worked with small groups of people. That was very difficult, in a way not finding the key. I think that's what we are always looking for. Hoping that fairly early on, you'll find something that will appear to be the sort of big clue as to where you're going.

That will make things unfold.

Yes. For example, early on in *Bloody Mess* we had this thing with the five of us. Rob and I dancing to some heavy metal music, Claire getting dressed up as a gorilla on one side of the stage, Cathy lying on the floor dead in the middle, and Terry crying over her. All done to the soundtrack of *Born to be Wild*. We made that on a Friday afternoon out of complete frustration with things. And what we loved about it was that you couldn't make any sense of it at all. It was like you were looking from one thing to the other thing in the picture, and you couldn't add them up. And we already had the title, *Bloody Mess*, and this thing was like a triangle, with the guys dancing, Cathy dead, Terry crying over her, Claire changing into the gorilla costume. And your eye would just go… [*looks from one thing to another*]. That really felt like the clue, because you wanted the show to be chaotic and very much back to collage, and so you just thought, 'Oh that's lovely. So what happens if we follow these two guys? What else do they want to do? What happens to Cathy? Does she really just lie dead during the show?' And finally, in the show she's the person who really wants her part to have a great big effect on people, but all her part ever consists of is lying down completely dead. So that thing, which can only be six minutes long because that's the length of the track – was the clue that broke open the whole show for us.

Because you get structure, you get stories, then you get themes.

Yes, you get places to lead from, I think. That's always what you're hunting for, this clue. And I think you know when you've found it. I can't explain why, but you do. Generally, you tend to like it because you don't quite understand what it is that you've made. There are other things that you do where you think it's nice, but you can see the logic of everything, and then somehow it's not very exciting to pursue it.

Do you think in some way the getting stuck-ness is also a necessary point in a process? That the show ends up getting better for it?

I think that's absolutely true. I don't think we've ever made anything where you don't get stuck.

Maybe it makes you go onto another level? Like the Friday afternoon craziness. Maybe you take your performance, or the way you think about the theme or the persons, to another level? Because you're sort of forced out of the pattern that you're thinking in.

I think that's true. Being stuck is in a way just falling into a pattern. In one way or another, you have to find a way to jolt yourself out of that. Yes, I think it's essential.

The other thing is that we tend to be very hard on material. We'll make something that we quite like, and then we'll say, 'Actually, if you were going to be mean about this, you would say that it was only this, this and this.' And being very harsh with what you've created is also important. The process of playing and making things and then afterwards talking, is almost as if you put a grid down on it and use it to say, 'Ok, really, what is this?' Then you have to take that off again and just mess about and make some more. So you're moving between two things, one is playing, and the other is analyzing what you're doing. Trying to intellectually project where it might go. And I think sometimes when you get stuck is when you get too much stuck in the talking. You find it impossible for days to get up and try anything because anybody can argue why it won't work. Do you know what I mean? It's like people can *prove* that that just won't work – while other people in the room are saying, 'Can we just try it? I don't care if it… Let's just try it, it will take us ten minutes and then we don't have to talk about it anymore.'

Dreams

What would you like to try out, if you could try anything in a work process?

I don't know. In a way, we can try anything, and that's what we're constantly faced with. So maybe the question is just what we would like to try? I think there's an interest for us in doing some work in a creative process with other people. More in terms of them coming and working with us, for example somebody leading a bit of work for a week. Or exposing us to different things. I think that would be useful.

If you could choose anybody in the world, or the history of theatre, who would you like or have liked to work with?

Jonathan Burrows, who's a dancer. Richard Maxwell. Meg Stewart, also a dancer. I'm interested in people from a dance background, because they're working with movement and that's something that we did a lot of, but it has really disappeared out of our work. I think there's an interest for us in trying to reengage with that in different ways.

But I find it very difficult to think about how you change the process. That's what we're quite interested in at the moment. And I think that exposure to other people's processes may be interesting for us. Though the process is such a private thing. I don't really believe in a methodology. I'm always rather suspicious of people who have a methodology. I think creating things is being a bit more haphazard.

But just exchanging what you do.

Yes, exactly. Seeing other things, hearing other people talk about their work is hugely interesting. Sometimes you get very cut off from that. Funnily enough, when you tour you don't see things, because you're always somewhere else when the show is on. Sometimes I think six months off where you just go and see things and talk to people would probably be very good.

Any other thoughts on utopian meetings?

I would have liked to have a conversation with Martin Scorsese – about thirty years ago – not now. When he was making work that I really liked. We used to say if we got stuck, what would so and so do in this situation? If you were Jan Fabre, what would you do now? Or if you were Needcompany, what would you do now? Or if you were Scorsese, what would you do now? Or if this was a film, and not a piece of theatre, what would happen? Or if this was music, what would happen next? If this was an album by The Fall, how would this work? Applying models that don't exist within theatre is just as interesting for us as applying ones that do.

Interview: Barbara Simonsen

Richard Lowdon (UK)
Richard Lowdon (born 1961) has a degree in Theatre Studies from Exeter University, and is a founding member, designer and performer in the experimental theatre company Forced Entertainment, formed in 1984. The award-winning and internationally acclaimed company creates mixed-media contemporary performances, installations, videos and durational performances.

Select works
Who Can Sing a Song to Unfrighten Me (1999)
Bloody Mess (2004)
Quizoola! (2013)
The Notebook (2014)

Website
www.forcedentertainment.com

14

Soheil Parsa

Why

What made you choose theatre? What is your first memory of theatre?

I think I was in my teen years when I got interested in theatre. I started in high school, playing in school shows, but it wasn't really serious. I was in love with basketball. I was a very good basketball player, so good that I was about to get on the provincial team. My coach was very hopeful that I might even make it to the national team, if I worked hard. So I was in love with basketball. But somehow, in grade eleven or twelve I got turned off by the whole environment, the sport mentality, the competitive, masculine atmosphere of the whole thing. But I was only doing theatre once in a while, as a hobby.

I was, I think, about twenty, when during summer I went to Tehran, the capital. My hometown is in the west of Iran, and at the time, my older brother was a student at Tehran University. He asked me if I wanted to see a movie called *Modern Times* by Charlie Chaplin. He said, 'Do you know him?' and I said, 'I've heard of him.' So I went and I saw the movie with my brother and it turned my life completely. I was so fascinated by the film. I'm not saying that immediately I knew this was my path of life, and that I had to become an artist. But I was really fascinated by that movie and I saw it twice that same week. And I think it was the beginning of my journey in theatre. The following year I applied for the theatre school in Tehran. I didn't get in. The competition was tough. The second year I failed again. They were only accepting seventeen to twenty people out of a thousand.

I realized that my knowledge about theatre was very small. I was a blond, handsome guy, with green eyes and long hair; I was thinking that I would be a superstar and act in the big movies, Iranian movies. But the message I got in the first two auditions was that I had little knowledge about theatre, I had to just go and learn. I had to read. So I had a year before I tried for the third time, and I started to read plays, Iranian, Western pieces, Bertolt Brecht, Chekhov, Stanislavsky. And the third time I got in. I was very happy. That was two years before the revolution.

At that time, you wanted to be an actor?

I wanted to be an actor, yes. I was trained as an actor. I had in those years a political mind, I was interested in poetry, I was interested in novels and stories. I think one of the reasons I was attracted to theatre was that I thought it could be an interesting 'social tool' to communicate something, say something, save humanity even. You know, naïve thinking of a teenage boy. It was not just that I wanted to be famous and become an actor; the intellectual aspect of the theatre fascinated me as well. I had that desire, that idea of doing something meaningful. But becoming famous was an important component of it as well!

Then the Iranian revolution happened, and for many different reasons I couldn't stay in Iran. I wasn't a political activist, but as a young guy, I was fascinated by socialism and even communism. It was young thinking, you know, it wasn't the real thing… And I had another serious issue, my family's religion. I'm not religious myself, but I come from a Bahai family, so that was another issue that I was faced with. They asked me to convert and change my name, in order to be allowed to stay and do my work. And it was a very tough decision. I felt that if I accepted changing my name and saying I was a Muslim, I was submitting to fascism somehow. I realized that staying in Iran would be impossible. I was young, I was about twenty-seven, and I decided it was time to leave. And I decided to celebrate the opportunity, all these difficulties facing me. I was really hungry to get out of the country, learn another language, pursue my dream and create theatre.

I escaped from Iran through the mountains and went to Pakistan. It took me about two years to get to Canada, and it was in 1984. In 1985, I started in the university theatre programme. I started from scratch. The main reason was to learn the language, and just be in the right environment, the theatre environment.

Did your relationship with theatre change much when you went to university in Canada, or was it a natural continuation?

No, it changed a great deal. The dominant concept for acting in Iran was still very much the Stanislavsky method. We also had courses about Iranian theatre, Japanese theatre. But it was interesting, when I came to Canada the distance from my culture made me more curious about it and especially the theatrical style of Iranian theatre. Because when you are within your own culture, you take things for granted. Ta'zieh is there, a traditional style of Iranian theatre. But when I came to Canada, the idea of a search has never left me. I'm always in search, always challenging myself. I barely spoke English at the age of twenty-nine. I had to start from scratch. I didn't take any acting or directing courses at university here, I went to theatre studies, so it was mainly theory. The courses I took in those years were mainly Japanese theatre, Asian theatre, and I was the one who introduced Iranian theatre to them, in one of my essays. They were very naïve, even one of the main universities in Canada, they had no idea. They had heard about Ta'zieh, for example, or Parde-Khani, but they had no idea, so I introduced them to it. At the same time, I got fascinated with the Western avant-garde.

I came from a very interesting time in Iran, before the Iranian Revolution, because Iranian theatre in those days was very, very active and alive. We had different kinds of theatre. We had the Art Festival of Shiraz – fantastic directors like Peter Brook, Grotowski and Richard Schechner came to Iran and performed there. It was a very vibrant theatre community, and we had some fantastic avant-garde Iranian directors. So I was familiar with avant-garde, Grotowski, all that. When I was in the first or second year at Tehran University, all these fantastic books like *Towards a Poor Theatre* and *The Empty Space* were translated into Persian, and we were swallowing them and discussing the concept and the ideals in these books. But coming to Canada was for me like a new start. I began as if I didn't know anything. Four years at university – forget it, put it aside, start from zero. And I had more material. If I wanted to do research on Grotowski, I had tons of material in English. Peter Brook, Meyerhold, Antonin Artaud, Edward Gordon Craig, all these people really fascinated me and really influenced me. And at the same time, I did a lot of research on the Japanese theatre and was fascinated by it. Noh and Kabuki, and Indian theatre.

So when you were studying in Iran it was really Western theatre that was the dominating trend, and the traditional Iranian theatre was something that you took for granted. But you must have memories about it?

Oh, absolutely. One of my most amazing memories is of Ta'zieh, the Iranian passion play. During my university years, we went to Isfahan, one of the cities in central Iran, and we all went to see a performance of Ta'zieh. We were all familiar with the story, a famous story in Islamic mythology; we knew what was going to happen. One of the children of the saint has been captured and taken away and they cut both his hands. And what they did in that performance was really breathtaking, I'll never forget it. The child was in the middle of this huge circle of people. Two horseback riders came in and the dust went up and there were 3,000 people sitting there watching this beautiful epic. One of them just picked up the child and passed it to the guy on the horse. And there were slogans and singing, like opera, and everyone… Then the rider disappeared behind the crowd. About thirty seconds later one hand, an artificial hand, all bloody, came surging from behind the audience. It was really very filmic. The hand was floating and rotating in the sky – and just fell down in the middle. And when it fell, the dust went up in a cloud. It was so powerful, everyone gasped. I'll never forget that moment. The magic of simplicity. How simple you can tell a story without being realistic and using a sword and trying to cheat the audience to believe you are cutting his hand. The technique was amazingly simple.

Images like that I think were very helpful to me. Especially when I did *Macbeth* [1995]. I used some techniques and ideas of the Ta'zieh. In Ta'zieh, a bowl of water represents a river or an ocean. It's a very codified language, like the Japanese Noh theatre, and if you bring it into theatre to a Western audience, it's ridiculous. It's not an ocean, it's a bowl of water. But in that culture of codified theatre, as soon as you bring a bowl of water the entire audience knows that it's the ocean or the river. The question for me was, can we do this in theatre? Using this idea and developing it, can we create an army with one person?

In *Macbeth* we created masks for our witches, fifteen of them, all black, one was red. They were made of stretchy fabric, one end attached to the floor, so at any time an actor could pick up this fabric and put it on his face like a bridle, and it was stretching, travelling. At one point, we had eight witches moving among each other with this stretchy fabric.

Again, in the process, time is so important. I remember we spent a complete four days to explore the idea of the witches. The first idea was umbrellas. For me the magical moment was how they could disappear. Theatre is not film. On film, they can disappear like that. How was this going to happen on stage? They were appearing and disappearing behind their umbrellas, and it was interesting, but they had to get rid of the umbrellas. And it was not really a mythic prop. Back and forth, we tried things, and finally, one night I went home and the idea came: suspenders. I used a sock and clipped on the suspenders. My son was about twelve years old and I asked him to come and put the sock over his eyes and start to move forward, while I was holding the suspenders. And I said, 'Let it go,' and he did, lifted it off, and it snapped back. That's what we used.

We had eight witches passing through the aisles among the audience. And at one moment, there was the sound of the fabric snapping back, and nobody was there. But it took us a full four days to discover this moment. A lot of people said that was Persian, but in the Persian culture we don't have witches. It was my creation, but I know that unconsciously this image comes from somewhere, from the culture. I just cannot point and say that's it.

How

About my process: all these elements that have influenced me since I left Iran indicate very strongly that I don't have a specific style. I refuse to have a style. At the beginning, when I was younger, I was in search of creating my signature and style. Gradually, I realized that I'm not interested in having that. I've learned that each process, each play, each production, requires its own way of doing things. I remember in the beginning I was imposing something – for example, I wanted to take Chekhov's *The Cherry Orchard* and totally stylize it the way I wanted it. It was in 1996 that we did the adaptation of that. And I realized that whatever we tried to do with Chekhov, it spit back in our face again. Why did I want to impose something on Chekhov? Something that doesn't come out of a necessity, doesn't come from the right place. It was that mentality that always you have to do something different and unique, change the world and say, 'Look how unique my approach is!'

I realized that the best and most unique approach to each piece is to find the essence of it, and find its spirit and communicate it. But of course, I must say I'm a bit biased against naturalism. I'm not really fascinated by that. My work hasn't been realistic or naturalistic. But in some productions I've had combinations of different styles.

The other thing I've found out about myself is that as soon as I get a little comfortable with one style, I challenge myself. I have a fear of repetition, of repeating myself. I don't know why, or if it's a good thing or a bad thing – and again, I don't want to push things. If I do a piece like *Waiting for Godot*, I want to make sure that it speaks to me and that I find my own way, very slowly going through it.

Canadian audiences have been surprised that each time, I come up with something different. Sometimes, you know, we have this tendency in every community that people want to label you. This is his style, that's the way he does things. And I've always defied that, I think, in my past twenty years of working in this country. That's a choice for me. I think there is a challenge for every artist to be honest, and just find out, what is my honest connection with this piece? Without bringing an interpretation. If there is an interpretation, it has to come from the world of the play, instead of me trying to impose something on it.

Do you have a certain structure for the rehearsal process, something that you always do?

Yes, I think there is a kind of method in the process. It's not a method for the style of the production, but there is a method. It is based on research and discovery. I don't go with too much structure in the rehearsal process, because I've always found that it works against me. It doesn't work. I get excited as soon as I see live people, actors there. That really inspires me. The moment I'm in the room, actors standing there, let's do this scene. With the limitations of funding, we have tried our best to really extend our process. It doesn't matter if it's a new play or it's a written play – I have to workshop, and that's not very common in Canada. When I did *Waiting for Godot* I had two weeks of workshop, and everybody was saying, 'Why? It's not a new play, why are you workshopping it?' Workshops are only for new plays. But my answer has always been, well, for me it's a new play. I have to find my own way of working, I have to discover the elements in this piece. I have to communicate with my actors. We have to find the style. As a director, you're not naïve. You have a sense, you have a hunch, you have an idea. And the whole process for me is exploring those initial ideas and developing a common vocabulary between myself, my designers and my actors. In a very early stage of the process I try to invite the designers, especially for sound. Lighting is more complicated, but I even invite them to come and see our workshops and see the process, the way we are talking. There comes a point where the moment is absolutely visual and I start talking about the lights, another layer.

One of my lighting designers that I really love, Andrea Lundy, once gave me a very interesting compliment. We were doing a show in 2006, *Bloom*, and for the last preview she wasn't available. She hired an assistant, another good lighting designer, and she told the assistant, 'Whenever you get confused about lighting, just watch Soheil's direction. By watching him you get a sense of the lighting.' I was very surprised. But I never sit in the rehearsal hall. I don't have a chair, I don't have a table, it doesn't work for me. I have to move with my actors, I have to be with them, I have to touch them, I have to feel them. And she said, 'Soheil, as soon as you start walking on the stage, even in the earliest rehearsal process, by watching your body movement I get a sense of the lighting.' I still don't understand why. But she does.

For example with a play like *Macbeth* or *Waiting for Godot*, I think we usually have one read-through and I refuse analysis. It stops me from being creative. If we analyse the scene and find out that it is about this – then get up and play it – then there is no other possibility, we made a decision, this is the choice, this is the scene and we have to play this. I always say to my actors, let's get on our feet and just do it. Just do it. *Then*, if necessary, we sit down and talk about it. For me, basically, each scene, each theatrical moment, is about conflict, is about the intention. It's always finding out what you are doing here. That's all. Let's try. Are you attacking people, so attack and see what happens. This scene, this man comes here, he wants this, okay, just do it. The philosophical meaning, the analysis, the subtext has to come out of that process. And it's amazing how much the actors get surprised when without any analysis they do it and then it feels right. Then we can sit down and talk.

But sometimes it's a big challenge, it depends on the training of the actors. Sometimes I face the difficulty that the person does not trust the process and says, 'I don't know, I have to sit down and talk about it.' But there's the benefit of the workshop. It is not only for me to see if the actors are suitable for the piece or not – they also have the choice to tell me, 'Soheil, sorry, it doesn't work. I don't like this process.' Sometimes that has happened. That's why we have the workshop, to establish that common vocabulary. It's about exploration.

I do the analytical work at home. But as soon as I walk to the theatre, the rehearsal space, it's totally intuitive. It doesn't work for me any other way. But the analytical work and your research, what you have done outside – it's there, it helps you unconsciously. Sometimes you do a scene, and you know it's not working, and sometimes as a director, I have a hard time explaining why. I don't have an intellectual response to it; I just know it's not working. We try it again. And we try it until finally we say, 'Yes, that's it.' So again, the process is about experimentation and discovery.

The essential

In your experience, what is the most important thing, the essential element that makes a good rehearsal process?

Openness – of the director and the actors. Total openness. No preconceived ideas.

The other element for me is time. Time is so important. It's as if, unconsciously, all human beings have a tendency to go towards the result and sometimes it's really hard to communicate that we don't have to rush. I say, slow down, we don't want to please anybody, let's explore. If something is not working, let's take our time, go back and revisit things.

So I would say openness and time. Especially openness is so important to me, because I consider myself a collaborator – and with no ego. I don't have a big ego at all. I've found that ego is the biggest enemy of the creative process. When it becomes about you or me and not about the work. I always try to communicate to my actors during the first few days that I'm not a god, I'm not entering the rehearsal hall as a god. I am the one who has to lead, and I'm going to make sure it happens, but let's explore and work together. It's all about the work. It's not about you or me.

I have such a great design team, and we know if something is not working it's not just because I'm the director and I say so – it's all about communication. My sound designer [Thomas Ryder Payne] will look at me and say, 'Soheil, you're not happy,' and I say no, and he says, 'Okay, I have another proposition.' That's how they all do. The final week is tech week, and it's the best part for me, because theatre is not just about telling a story through the text. It's so fun for me to start playing with these elements. Andrea, my lighting designer, usually comes and says, 'Okay Soheil, this is what you have.' We sit down for half an hour and she shows me everything. And she shows me her ideas for this scene and that moment. Then we start playing and revisiting the things that are not coming across properly. I'll say, 'Can we make this a touch darker, I need a silhouette here,' and she says, 'This is too dark, it doesn't make the contrast with the previous' and so on. It's a really fun process. And we've established that agreement that it's not about you and me, and they all know that. They feel it and they know that I'm honest when I say something is not working. Andrea will say, 'Let's stop everything, what do you see in your mind?' I say, 'I see just that light and the chair, and the silhouette in the other corner and that's all.' She says, 'That's a bit difficult, but I'll show you.' Then I realize that it needs another element to make that picture really clear. So it's all about communication, giving and taking, questioning, and no ego.

Problems

I think you've already answered the question, what is the biggest problem or obstacle in the rehearsal process?

Ego.

Anything else that always seems to come up and is difficult to solve?

Yes, sometimes… A really frustrating thing for me is that I know the scene, and I know the character, and I know the moment, but for some reason I can't find the right word and the vocabulary to communicate, and the actor doesn't get it. And you *know* it goes on. For example, *Waiting for Godot* was a successful production. People loved it, people found it seamless, beautiful, funny, time passed by quickly, they never felt bored. But I remember at least three or four moments that never got resolved, and it pained me so much.

It wasn't because the actors resisted, just something – that communication, that clarity never happened. Sometimes that's the worst thing, you try a hundred different things and still the actors don't get it. Sometimes it comes down to one line, and I hate doing a line reading, but sometimes you feel like you know how this line has to be said. You don't want to just do a line reading, because you have to trust the actor. A couple of times I've had to say, 'If you don't mind, that's the way I hear it, this is the line.' It worked. But sometimes whatever you do it doesn't work.

I think that obstacle is always there. Always. I've never had any production where everything I see is perfect – it's impossible. And I think that's the beauty of it, it pushes you to go somewhere else and question the next production. But as you continue working, you find that vocabulary. And especially if you work with the right actors, the right artistic team, of course it makes it easier and easier.

Dreams

If you could change or try out anything in the rehearsal process, do anything you dream about, what would that be?

My dream is to get heavily subsidized and for example do *Hamlet* with six months of endless exploration of everything and with my complete design team, in a real theatre, with the lights from the first day, sound, props and set. Having the benefit of lighting, set, costumes, sound design, and still having the time to explore everything, do a scene and be actors-director only. Just find the moment of this scene, let's get the light, let's play it, stop, and let the lighting designer just put up the ladders and go and fix the light.

That's my dream. Because as I said, I'm not really a text person. Theatre for me is absolutely a combination of all these elements. Having that luxury even for four weeks would make me very, very happy. Because a design element really changes the direction and may change the text. When suddenly you discover a fantastic visual moment that tells a lot of story you may just cut three pages. I'm very, very visual, but I don't sit at home and figure out how I am going to make a certain moment visual – it happens, that's my vocabulary. But that would be my dream.

Interview: Barbara Simonsen

Soheil Parsa (CA)
Soheil Parsa (born 1954) was born in Iran and studied acting and theatre at the University of Tehran. After coming to Canada in 1984, he completed a second Bachelor of Arts in Theatre Studies at York University and established Modern Times Stage Company, an experimenting, culturally diverse and award-winning theatre company.

Select works
Macbeth (2005)
Aurash (2009)
Forgiveness (2013)
The Death of the King (2016)

Website
www.moderntimesstage.com

15

Diane Paulus

Why

Why did you choose theatre or how did you end up in theatre?

I grew up in New York City as a kid, and I was lucky enough to be exposed to a lot of arts when I was young. I regularly went to the theatre; I was taken to Broadway shows when I was a little girl. I also studied music and I played the piano very seriously, and I studied ballet. And I had this incredible opportunity when I was a little girl to dance with New York City Ballet as one of their child performers. I was nine, ten and eleven, but I was there doing the *The Nutcracker*, *Coppélia*, *A Midsummer Night's Dream*, *The Firebird*, when [George] Balanchine was still alive. So some of my earliest memories of the professional theatre were watching Balanchine deal with Suzanne Farrell and Patricia McBride and all these incredible ballet stars. And of course Balanchine was so known for his story ballets, so watching how he told story through movement was a huge influence on me. I grew up also in a family that really lived and breathed the arts. I had an older sister who was a professional harpist so we had a harp in our living room, and my father had been an actor when he was young and then went into television. But he actually was directing plays for the United States Army Entertainment corps during the American occupation of Japan, where he met my mother who was Japanese. And one day I was digging through boxes of my parents' things, and I saw a picture of my father in the Stars and Stripes army newspaper with a play in his hand, and the article said, you know, 'Larry Paulus pulling his hair out, because the show is on tonight and how is he going to get it done in time?' And it was the first show he was doing in Tokyo during the occupation, and I had this moment of thinking, 'Of course this is what I do.' When I became an adult my dad wasn't doing theatre, he was producing live television for CBS, so I didn't know my father as a theatre person and then when I dug out this memorabilia of my dad being a director it made total sense to me.

So I was really exposed to theatre and the arts all growing up. I had a family who understood the value of the arts and loved the arts. When I went to college, though, I thought I was going to go into politics. I was very motivated to study government, I wanted to be the mayor of New York, that was one of my dreams. I spent my first summer after my freshman year at college working for a city council member from my Upper West Side district. And it was actually in that summer that I had a light-bulb moment where I was sent by the politician, Ruth Messinger, to this Coalition for the Homeless meeting, and I was asked to attend on her behalf to tell everyone that 'Council member Ruth Messinger supports your cause.' So I was eighteen years old and I sat in this meeting and said what I was supposed to say. And then they went on to discuss how they were going to get the food to the homeless people. They had van routes, they were taking out chalk and the chalk-board – and I just remember feeling that I wanted to be in their shoes. I wanted to be in the trenches. I wanted to be having contact with making something happen in a different way rather than the one step removed. God knows politicians have to shake a lot of hands and they are critical to making change in our lives, but there was something about this notion of being in the trenches that I realized I am addicted to. This art of making the impossible possible with a group of people. And when I was studying piano as a young girl I was a very good piano player and my teacher wanted me to pursue it professionally and go to Juilliard, and I was maybe at that time twelve years old. And I also remember thinking, 'I don't want to do this, because I don't want to be by myself'. I understood what it would mean to be a serious concert pianist. I would have to practise four to five hours a day by myself, and sometimes I think to this day that if I had picked an orchestral instrument like a violin I might be a musician today. Because that orchestral experience is so satisfying as a group experience. But somehow the piano felt very lonely. And I had dipped my toes into a performance through being a child dancer with the New York City Ballet, and I was doing theatre at my school; I saw what that group dynamic was. And I knew in my heart that's where I want to be.

Did you always want to direct?

You know, I trained as an actor. But I trained as an actor knowing that that's the fundamental language of the theatre. So I think I always thought to myself, if I don't end up being an actor, knowing the ABCs of acting will help me whether I become a director, a producer or whatever I want to do. I had another very significant experience as a young actor. I graduated acting school and I got headshots done, which a lot of young people do. And I actually got a meeting with an agent, so I thought, well, this is all working out well. And the agent looked at the headshots and she said, 'Oh, you're so exotic-looking, tell me what your background is.' And I was a young, eager actor so I said, 'Well, I'm half Japanese, my mother's Japanese.' And she said, 'Ah, *that's* why you look like a Vietnamese bar girl in these headshots. We're going to have to redo them.' And I was very young and eager so I said, of course, and she said, 'We'll pay for them, we're going to send you back, we're going to redo your headshots.' So they sent me back to this photographer. They curled my hair. My hair is straight like this, to this day, twenty years later, my hair is long and straight like this. I did these headshots, they came back curly and she loved them and I made two thousand copies of that picture and made postcards – in those days, this was the early nineties, you made them with a service number, so you were literally putting out your picture with a telephone number. And I remember picking up the postcards – and I put them in a shopping bag and I don't think I ever took them out again, and I knew this was not why I loved the theatre, this was not why I wanted to be in this profession.

So there were several moments for me where I realized… I adore actors, I will do anything for an actor, I really believe actors go through so much for their art, and I will worship at the shrine of the actor, but I realized I could not be an actor. There was something about the creative impulse and having control over what you want to do, what you want to say, what the theatre can mean in the world that traditionally in the hierarchy – not always, but traditionally – the actor is not in that driver's seat. So there was something for me about becoming a director that made me feel empowered to integrate everything I believed in, politics, social change, community building. These are why I do the theatre. That I could harness all those passions through being a director, more powerfully.

How

Can you try to describe a typical rehearsal process for you?

When I think about rehearsal, that's really a very mature moment for a director, because you've done so much prior to that first rehearsal. You have to fall in love, so to speak, with your project, you have to date it and learn everything about it and go through many ups and downs before you even enter your first day of rehearsal. And then I feel like when I finally get in rehearsal with actors, my job on the first day is to spread my obsession. I've been obsessed with this material sometimes a year, two years, three years. It's been in my subconscious, I've been dreaming about it, I've been researching it, I've been developing it with my creative team. Now I have to enter the room with a team of performers and say, *this* is why we need to reach beyond, this is why this process ahead of us is necessary, this is why we're here.

And usually on day one I find, now having done this several times, that people are nervous, they are uncomfortable, and sometimes as a director what you can do more than anything is get people to relax, get people to feel open. I always say on my first day of rehearsal: 'I'm going to bring an idea to the table. I expect you to bring an idea to the table. But I'm looking for the third idea that is better than either of our ideas.' And I find that's really important to say up front, because it puts the actor in a creative headspace. You know, as directors, sometimes people think that we want actors to do what we tell them to do. This idea of the actor as a puppet, that that's your dream experience when the actors just do what the director wants. That is my nightmare. Truly. You know, when an actor says, 'What do you want?' I don't know what I want. What I know I have are questions. And I always say to young directors who come to me, 'Don't worry about having to have the answer. Actually, you shouldn't know the answer. The whole process of the entire production – preproduction, rehearsal, even with an audience – is to discover the answer to your question.' But you have to have a question. And I've always felt the work will be more deep, more fulfilling, the bigger the question is. The issue becomes: Are you asking a big enough question?

So the beginning of rehearsal is about getting everyone as excited as I am, transferring that obsession, making the actors, particularly the actors… Because I think in America we live in a very hierarchical creative environment, we are not the beneficiaries of a more European, company-based ensemble approach. It's much more work for hire. So an actor arrives, they're worried about being fired, they want to do the right thing. They're nervous. And I know as a director that the work is going to be better and deeper if *everyone* in the room cares as much as I care. That's not just the actor, that's the stage manager, that's the intern sitting to my left, it's the production assistant. I want to create an environment where everybody is thinking, how can we make this better? How can we solve that problem?

So more of an ensemble environment, in fact. How do you do that, concretely?

I think you try to create an environment which really shows that people's opinion will be valued and listened to. Because it's typical as a leader, whether you're in the theatre or in a business, to say, 'We want to know what everybody thinks,' but then no one says anything, because they don't really believe you care. You have to really create that environment. If an actor says, 'How about this?', you have to say, 'Well great, let's try it.' And I often say in a process, 'Option A. Let's go.' We'll go through option A and then say, 'Great, let's put that here. Now let's try option B. Oh, someone's got option C, well let's try that.' So you really lay out that we're trying many options, there are many ways to solve a problem. And then of course as a director you need to guide. You can't let it become chaotic, because actors and everyone will panic, if they think the director doesn't know what he or she is doing. So you look and you watch and like a great editor you can say, 'I think option B works best, so let's stick with that.' And sometimes it's good to say, 'For today, let's stick with B. Let's see as we go, maybe we'll learn more.' Often in a production you're learning the vocabulary, you're learning the storytelling, so sometimes if you micromanage too much on one moment you'll beat it to death. So you come at it in maybe three or five different ways, and then it's time to move on, let it go. Do the rest of the work, and then you find when you come back you'll know exactly what you need to do.

How much rehearsal time do you normally have?

Actual rehearsal time with the acting company full on, typically on a musical which is what I have been doing, is five to six weeks. And that's on the generous side. Usually five weeks. Four weeks I find impossible. And prior to that rehearsal period you definitely have at least one week of preproduction where you're in the studio with your choreographer and several dancers working out vocabulary. Prior to that on a musical you've definitely had at least one physical workshop which is two to three weeks where you're working out, hopefully with some of the actors. You know, the best way to develop a musical is that you cast it and go through several phases of a reading, a second reading, a physical workshop with the choreographer, and then you hit rehearsal. So when you look at your rehearsal period being five to six weeks you really actually have to include everything that's part of the preproduction. And that's why I love doing musicals, because

I find that in the American musical theatre we understand that a musical takes this kind of development. So oddly, even though the American musical can be looked at as the flashiest, most entertaining, commercial product of the American theatre I know, having been inside it, that it has the most development process of all the forms.

It comes with the territory, so much that it's what's the best practice, what's the normal practice. It's all about resource, about what you're willing to invest in the development. What we have been doing at the ART, which is the American Repertory Theater at Harvard where I'm the artistic director, is that we incubate new musicals. We will do a reading, a second reading, a workshop, and then we do an entire production with five weeks of rehearsal, two weeks of tech, three weeks of previews where we're making changes every day, and then we run it another five weeks. And when that's over, we go back into a creative mode, to plan more changes if the show moves to Broadway. Then when we move to Broadway we might have another workshop, and another five-week rehearsal period, previews and opening. That's why when they are given that length of development they stand a chance. At ART we don't look at ourselves as an out-of-town try-out for Broadway. We are a not-for-profit theatre dedicated to expanding the boundaries of theatre. And one of the ways that we love to do that is building and stimulating the most ground-breaking American new musicals we can. We hope to birth that in a safe environment for artists. For instance with *Waitress* [ART 2015; Broadway 2016, directed by Paulus] you have a pop composer, Sara Bareilles, who's never written for the musical theatre. She has the opportunity to come to ART to really cut her teeth, to try things. When things go directly to Broadway it's very, very difficult. It's a commercial environment where you have very little time and the risk is much higher. So starting at a theatre where you can really develop something, especially in front of an audience… So when you ask me, what's rehearsal, let's say for a show that I'm doing in Broadway it begins two years earlier in a theatre like the ART. That's really the beginning.

Are all of your rehearsal weeks in a rehearsal hall or also in the theatre space?

When you're in a rehearsal period for a musical that is five or six weeks that's exclusively in the rehearsal hall. You're usually rehearsing in three different spaces doing multiple things every day. You have your one main room where you're blocking the play, and everything is set out on the floor, and you're moving chronologically through the narrative. You try as best you can to have everything at real scale. And then you'll have a second space, hopefully as large, with the stage marked out, so that things can be taken into a second space while you are continuing: numbers, dance numbers, scenes. And then you have a third space, usually where you're practising music all the time. So you're sort of multitasking on three cylinders. And usually you have to have another space for your composer, because you are actually asking your composer during this five-week process to make changes. So now I know when I do any musical that I ask for four spaces. Sometimes they're closets and we can make do with a closet, but you need that amount of space, because the productive, creative changes that are happening are so enormous.

That's what never ceases to amaze me about process. You think you know everything and then you get in the room, in real time and space, and the next level of discovery happens. And then of course when you leave the rehearsal and move on stage things are going to change. So I always say to actors a phrase that I learned from one of my great mentors, the Romanian director Andrei Șerban: 'Hold on tightly. Let go lightly.' Because as an artist, whether you're the actor, the costume designer or anyone involved, of course there are things we're holding on to. You have to. Otherwise there'd be chaos. But then you have to learn to let go. Always. You let go in rehearsal, you let go when you hit the stage and all of a sudden realize that that whole scene that was over there at that table has to be moved over here. Because it just doesn't feel right in the space. So it's a constant process of change. I find that the more you can communicate why you're making the change, again making the actors not just the recipients of 'move here, do this', but making them understand why you're doing what you're doing, they'll go along. They will meet you more than halfway. They'll start to problem solve. That's my greatest moment in rehearsal whether you're in the hall or on the stage, when the actor says, 'I know how to fix it. How about this, Diane? I'll cross here and then I'll pick up the sponge', and I say, 'Perfect.' Because there comes a time in the process where the actor knows more than you do. You're waiting for that moment and waiting for the actor to tell you, because they're inside it and they know more than you.

Do you find that during the whole of those five or six weeks you are able to use the 'method' of options A, B and C, or does it naturally close more and more?

You are definitely building and zeroing in on the structure and the benchmarks that you need to set for your storytelling. And so much of being a director and guiding a process is about feeling the time of the rehearsal and where you need to get. It's an intuitive understanding that we need to deliver this by this date, and some actors are there earlier than others so you have to support those that are going quickly, but also not panic the ones that need more time. But I'll tell you, even when you get quite advanced in your process, in some ways the more you know the more the things that are off become even more clear when they are off. So it's not uncommon even when you're down to, say, a final run-through, you see your first run-through and you go, 'Okay, now I know. We have to completely redo the beginning.' And you go back to the drawing board. But you're not throwing everything out. You're building.

So it's a process I find… The rehearsal hall is controlled chaos. Mark Rylance, who is a great actor that we just worked with at the ART, said something that really resonated: That the more he is in the theatre the more he realizes that the longer he can stay in the chaos, that's the key. And he said in his beautiful, poetic way, 'Because unless you're in the compost heap you never have a chance at really having the beautiful tree come out of the mess.' So for me rehearsal is about creating that environment that can feel chaotic – I know I can handle it, and I have to gauge to what degree every actor can handle it, some can really handle chaos, others get nervous – that environment where you are not closing down too quickly. Trying to stay open to the accident, to the surprise, to the better idea. And then sometimes you say, 'Let's leave this for now'. Maybe we know, maybe I know it's not right. But we're going to leave it, and I know that I will have a shot at a better idea once we hit the theatre. So you're constantly guiding and choosing when to make a change.

The essential

What is in your experience the essential condition for a rehearsal process to go well, to be successful?

That's a very good question. I'm very adamant about inviting people into a process who I feel are there for the right reason. So my answer to your question about what is essential starts actually with who is in the room. And now, whenever I audition an actor for a show, even if they are fantastic, and they can sing, and act, and do everything better than anyone, I always ask, 'Can we speak to someone who has worked with this person?' Can I find out from a director, or a stage manager, or a producer if they are in it for the greater good, for the company. Are they a good company member? Are they a 'good egg'? Because it's so hard. Rehearsal is hard. If we're going to be truly creative we have to be able to lose ourselves in a process. We have to be willing to risk not knowing the answer if we really want to make something great. So if someone is hung up on themselves in a certain way, it can really be a Dutchman. That can be the hardest obstacle in rehearsal. No matter what I say, if that person is stuck in a way it's very hard in a process to change someone. Sometimes it happens, which is great, or someone will learn how to work in a new way. But I find rehearsals will go well when everyone has come into the process with a clean understanding that this is the way we're going to work. This is the goal, this is the kind of project, this is the kind of spirit in which we're going to work. And again, because we are not in a European system of a company or repertoire you almost have to build the company every time. You have to take the time and energy to make sure that you're putting the right people. That's not only your actors, that's your stage managers, your creative team, your choreographers, designers. Everyone has to share the philosophy of the way we're going to work, which for me is a collaborative, deeply ego-less group experience. And if people aren't up for that, you know, maybe it's not right for them. I find most people love the theatre because they love to be in a group. They love that group experience. So it's not that hard to make that invitation happen, but it's an important moment, I think, to make sure everybody is jumping off the cliff together with that understanding.

Problems

What is in your experience the biggest problem that comes in the rehearsal process – that you can't avoid, that always comes up, that is hardest to solve?

In every rehearsal process you're going to hit major challenges. The more you do it the more you realize that actually, you can't panic when the challenge comes. Growing up and getting experience you realize there is no process by definition that will be smooth sailing. What is different in every process is that the problem comes in a different area. Sometimes it's a difficult producer, sometimes it's the estate of the writer who is no longer living, maybe they become difficult, or maybe it's one of the actors. There is always going to be some drama coming somewhere. So I actually feel if it's going too well and there are no problems, that's when I get panicky, because I think 'Something's coming, this is not right.' I think the more you do the theatre the more you realize and you learn to trust that when it's difficult, when there is really friction you can't check out of it, you have to just keep going. Because sometimes at the hardest moment where things are the most tense, or you're hitting rock bottom – and that can be any number of things, whether it's a creative problem, whether it's a rewrite on a script that's not happening, whether there is a performer that's stuck and just not delivering – in a way the more you can live with that tension, enter it, continue to work through it, the more you stand the chance to really hit the breakthrough. You do learn sometimes if there is some aspect of a process where the energy is so negative, sometimes you have to realize it and you remove it. That's the hard decision that you hope you never have to make. But that's what you're evaluating. Difficult times – bring 'em on. It's not milk and cookies. That's what Andrei Şerban used to always say, when I was a young director trainee, 'There are some people who bring milk and cookies to rehearsals, but I'm not one of them.' And I think I'm more of the Andrei School. I know it's going to be tough and if it's milk and cookies then it's going to be banal art, right? So let the problems come.

But you think that it has to do with people, the problems that always come up.

I do. When you really hit a roadblock it will be because of an energy from a person where it is so negative and it has nothing to do with the process. They're stuck in something and it's detrimental to the process.

What can you do?

In that situation you try to work through it. Any number of ways. You try to define the process, you try to communicate in a different way, whether it's with an actor, a producer or a designer, because God knows we all want to continue together, and as a director I feel my job is to get the best work out of everyone. Coach. If someone's stuck I'm going to try to release them to a greater sense of their work. But if it's just hostile energy, after three or four tries sometimes you have to make a change. And you really don't resort to that unless it's really necessary. But a lot of process is having faith. You really have to get the room, your team, your collaborators, your actors to know that there is light at the end of the tunnel. They may not feel it, that's why people get scared, because they're in it and they're thinking, this can't be, I don't know what I'm doing. And you have to let people feel it's okay, you're on the way. Hold on, let go – hold on tightly, let go lightly – trust, we will get there. You have to be like a hands-on coach.

Dreams

If you could change anything about a rehearsal process, or try out anything, what would you want to do?

I've actually been thinking lately how gratifying it would be to work with a group of people like a company on multiple projects. So that you don't have to reinitiate the process every time. That's what I do as a director in our American system, you spend a lot of energy getting the group to be like a company that's played together for years. I think my dream right now, as I think about the creative place I'd like to live in, would be: Wouldn't it be great if you just had that company? So that when you begin again – because the theatre is about beginning again and again – you begin at that mutual understanding. I had a company when I was a young director, and I know that there are other kinds of problems [*laughing*] that come when you are years and years together in a company. For me it's finding that balance.

I actually think a little more rehearsal time would be healthy, but I like it over time. I think if I were given twelve weeks of rehearsal I might start going like this [*circling with a finger*]. The pressure sometimes pushes you. But having the adequate development time over two years to me that is necessary. Having a shot at creating the whole production and then go back to the rehearsal room. *That* is something I would love more of a chance at. When you've done it, and you've seen it in front of an audience and you say, 'Now I understand. Get me back in the rehearsal room.' That's what I would love to do more of.

Interview: Barbara Simonsen

Diane Paulus (US)

Diane Paulus (born 1966) is a director of theatre and opera. She graduated from Harvard University in Social Studies and has a master's degree from Columbian University School of the Arts. Paulus is artistic director of the ART (American Repertory Theater) at Harvard University since 2009. She has directed numerous Broadway musicals and was nominated for the Best Director Tony Award for her revival of *Hair*, and won the award in 2013 for her revival of *Pippin*.

Select works

The Donkey Show (1999)
Hair (2008)
Pippin (2012)
Waitress (2016)

Website

www.dianepaulus.net

16

Catherine Poher

Why

How did you get into theatre?

It must have been when I was very young. I think I was fourteen years old, when I went to see Ariane Mnouchkine in Paris. I don't remember the name of the performance, but they had made these mountains. And what I remember was that at the end of the performance all the actors were standing at the top of the mountains waving. Waving goodbye to the audience. But I did not want to leave. I felt like, 'This is my family. I belong here.' I started to cry and I wanted to climb up the mountains and stay there with them. I think that's where it began.

After that I started going to the theatre a lot. It was back in the 1970s (and 1980s) when all the big names came to Paris. Bob Wilson, Meredith Monk and Pina Bausch: *Café Müller*. And Peter Brook with *Mahabharata* and *La conférence des oiseaux*. Huge theatrical experiences. The Bread and Puppet Theatre came too. There was so much, so I crammed myself with theatre. I was still in high school at the time.

Then I went to dance workshops and I signed up for a course in mime. Every Saturday I attended an entire day of mime. I didn't particularly enjoy being on stage myself, but I went to these workshops. At one point we were a group of hippies with a total dictator – I don't even remember his name – and we were trying to do these deep experimental things, throwing ourselves out of windows in pavilions outside Paris, and making happenings. I was still very young, seventeen or eighteen.

When I left high school and went to art school in Paris I saw an advertisement for summer courses at a folk high school for arts in

Figure 5 Barbara Simonsen and Catherine Poher, Copenhagen, February 2010

Holbæk, Denmark. So I went there. There I met Kirsten Dehlholm[1] – she was my teacher in textile design, and we became good friends. She visited me a couple of times in Paris where I had changed from painting to architecture, and I visited her in Copenhagen. Then one day she called me up and said, 'I'm starting the Theatre of Images [Billedstofteatret], won't you come up? You've almost finished studying anyway.' And I thought, 'Why not?' It seemed like a really good idea, especially since I had just received my diploma in architecture. And I had had this little letter in my mailbox from one of my examiners. He had made the effort of finding me and delivering a letter that said, 'Please don't stop playing. It has been a pleasure to see your work. Don't grow up, keep playing.'

So I thought, okay, I'll go to Copenhagen. I came in 1977 and thought that I would stay for a couple of years to play with Kirsten and then go back. That was thirty-three years ago. We started Billedstofteatret, and we were a basic group of eight, I think. We made big site-specific performances, something very unusual back in 1977. From then on it just continued. And I also stayed in Denmark because I fell in love and had a family.

So even though you had seen theatre as a teenager and knew that that was what you wanted to do, still you went to art school and not theatre school?

No, because I wasn't interested in traditional theatre. I wasn't interested in the things that you could learn to do there, although I did look into those theatre schools. I was too old to start dancing. Besides, in those days dance was still very much based on ballet. And someone like Bob Wilson was an architect, so you didn't have to… I also didn't make a conscious choice to be a theatre person. It was a place where I felt good, but I was more of a painter. That was where I felt at home. I've always drawn and painted. I started an education as a painter, but I was very politically active, and at the time painting and art were bourgeois virtues, so it didn't go well with my political values. I thought I would study architecture and make social housing. I'm glad I studied architecture, because I still use it when I work with spaces.

How

Can you tell me about a typical method or rehearsal process of yours? Are there some basic elements you always use, or can you give examples of specific processes?

I think what is typical for me is that it's never typical. Because every work has its own logic and its own language. I don't think I have had two processes that were the same, and I've created or collaborated in about seventy performances. So each time it's very, very different.

For example, *Ta' Ti Ting* [*Take Ten Things*] with Theatre Rio Rose [2002]. It all started in an aeroplane when I went to Burma – or Myanmar, as it's called now – and there was a Japanese man sitting next to me. He said, 'Let me show you what I have found.' And then he rolled out a small bag filled with small diamonds and gemstones. He was a buyer and was going back to Japan with what he had bought. He told me about all the different gems, and then he rolled up the little bag again, took up another bag, rolled it out, and in it was an ancient book that he started to read. I asked him, 'What are you reading?' and he said, 'I'm reading Tao Te Ching, and it is a fantastic thing, because every time I've finished reading it I can start over again, because it has changed.' He laughed and just went on reading.

And I thought, 'Of course.' If it's a really wise book, he will have changed so much when he has finished reading it that he can start again and go a little deeper. It's an eternal reading process, the rest of his life. I would like to read that book, I thought. When I came home, there was just one of these serendipities or coincidences of life. They had just made a new Danish translation of Tao Te Ching, and it was in all the shop windows. I bought it and read it, and thought, wow! This text is so rich, I want to work with it.

I talked to Tove Bornhøft [artistic director of Theatre Rio Rose] and we got together a team. We wanted several generations, so one of them was an elderly lady, and I also wanted as many different theatre languages as possible. So we had Tove, who was from the Odin Theatre tradition; Folmer Kristensen, who was from a circus artist tradition; Jakob Haahr, who was a Pina Bausch-dancer; and Kim Mühlenfeldt, who was a Royal Theatre classical ballet dancer. Then there was Joakim Eggert, a young musician with a good sense of rhythm; and our elderly lady who just had to be. Which is the hardest.

We read the texts over and over and over, and discussed and worked out some questions. We had a week or ten days together, and while we were reading we would play. I made all kinds of themes for improvisations, and some of the others did too, and we collected material. For me it was about finding out how we could make a unity out of all the different expressions, because I wanted to make one world. In the world we are all very different, but we make a unity. And the stage for me is like the world in a concentrate. Like super strong coffee. And I don't mean semi-strong coffee or bad coffee, I mean really, really strong.

So how could each of them be the strongest version possible? During those ten days I got a sense of what was working and not working, and then I continued on my own, working with the visual part of it. How could I make it so that even though there are only six of us we seem like the whole world? I was very inspired by a French installation artist called [Christian] Boltanski, who worked with memories, for example by using lots of clothes – shelves filled with clothes. I thought, I'll make a floor of clothes, and we'll improvise with that. For the first day of improvisation there were eight square metres of clothes and the characters came out of that. I could see in the improvisations that the clothes were both memory and also a sort of nest, when you push it together. To me, a nest is a symbol of being inside the womb. And when you collect all the stories you arrive at myths and fairy tales. It is like going into the world of fairy tales. The clothes would form a bed, and they could become a coffin. With just this one element that you could push into various forms, you were able to tell the story of a whole life.

So it all started by chance in an aeroplane, and then with a meeting between a group of people. Inside that group of people there is a secret, and that is what to me is so fantastic. What is the secret in there, in exactly that constellation? That is what I'm looking for. What is it that we – exactly these people – are able to create? You have to be able to let go of your control, and you have to have a deep, deep belief in chaos. You have to be able to be in that. Instead of calling myself director I would like to call myself 'chaos-container'. That's how I experience myself. I have to be able to be in chaos in order to give that sense of security to everybody else. Because it is very, very fear-provoking, not knowing where you are going. I don't give out a manuscript. That's very rare.

When will there begin to be a structure, typically?

That varies a lot. Sometimes I may have an idea of a structure. There will be a kind of skeleton quite early on. In *Haiku* [1998], for example, very early there were the four seasons, and a man and a woman. The woman was carrying eternity and the man was carrying the moment. In Haiku poems you have an element of eternity and an element of now. But at other times there is no skeleton at all. It won't be until the end of the process that I suddenly go, 'Ahh!'

In *Ta' Ti Ting* it was quite late that I found out that we could give all the material that we had to the audience. The frame we made was that it was the memories of the old woman, and that she was dying. We are actually looking at the last thing. She is sitting there at a nursing home eating her soup, and everything that happens is the embodiment of something that has happened in her life. We are embodying her memories.

It came one day out of the blue. You must always find a key. You make all sorts of material and then there has to be a key. A key that you find to make the audience go along a certain road with you. It is as if you have to have the first point of departure where you make a kind of deal with your audience. Then they can relax and they can receive. If you don't make it, the audience will spend all their energy thinking, 'Well, and what does that mean?' instead of letting it come. I really enjoy turning off the head. The head is very good afterwards. When you have experienced the performance and you have been completely bombarded, then you can come home and think and discuss. But that is afterwards. If I'm sitting at a performance thinking, I don't see anything. If I'm thinking, 'So, how did they do this and that? Is that a filter or something?' – then I don't experience it.

That is what I try to do and it is really difficult. It is not very often that it works. I try to make it so that what you see is so much a matter of course that you don't have to speculate.

Do you remember where the key of the old woman came from?

I think I suddenly thought, 'That's how I can make the whole group work.' That she was the key. Because she was so fantastic in her presence and her matter-of-factness – she was just there. Immediately, when you saw her, you wanted to be with her, and you felt interested. From then on you could do anything. The first image of the performance is that she pulls the young dancer out of the clothes and you didn't know that anyone was inside the clothes. Up he comes all naked and then he creates the history of the human race just by changing his underwear. And it was because she had that presence that you were able to make these total clashes of images that would open up. Where anything can happen. Anything can happen.

Can you describe the process of making The Comical Tragedy *[1993]?*

Yes, that was interesting. Hans Rønne [actor and director] and I had already done three or four shows together. And they were very physical. Extremely. We had developed a kind of language that would describe mental states through actions. It was something we had worked out together. And we had long talks about how it could be fun to challenge ourselves and try out new directions, but we didn't really know what. But while I was touring in France – that was when I was still performing – I saw *The Comical Tragedy* played by the original artist, Yves Hunstad.[2] And I thought, 'That's Hans. That's totally Hans.' I asked Yves if we could buy it and he agreed. He already had five other people around Europe performing it.

But at the same time, Hans had also heard about this play from a Swedish colleague. Again, the strange coincidences of life. So, when I came to him and said, 'Hans, Hans, I've found this piece,' he said, 'How odd! I've heard about it too.' We bought the manuscript, and we read it over and over, and we thought, 'Good heavens, all those words!' All this text. What are we going to do about it? We were in a sweat, because I couldn't work with text, I didn't know how, and neither could he. He couldn't get three words out of his mouth.

We started by cutting. We cut away half an hour, actually. And we asked [director] Lane Lind for help. We spent a day with her going through the whole text, where she helped us analyse and find the intentions etc. And we thought, okay, here we go. I told Hans, 'You know, we'd better not work with that text. We'll figure out what the scene's content is and then you'll speak gibberish. It doesn't matter what you say, we'll make body language.' That's how we worked. Scene after scene, where Hans was just speaking gibberish. We went through the entire performance like that. Then little by little, we added language. And every time it was like adding a stone to it. It was very difficult. We did a few showings at the folk high schools in the area, and all the kids fell asleep. Like, snoring: 'When is it finished?' We were desperate and thought it would never work.

But we are stubborn. And it was always like that for Hans and me. All our first showings were always total failures. We had that experience. Just because we make failures during the work process it doesn't mean that it will be a failure at the end. So we just kept on and on, and Hans got more and more on top of the text. Until suddenly he forgot the text, because he had it in his body, and poof! There was a beautiful performance. That's how we tamed it.

The essential

What is the most important thing for the rehearsal process to succeed and for a good performance to come out of it? What is the most important thing needed for the process?

Trust. It is hugely important that the people involved have trust in each other. That requires that everyone does the work they are supposed to. That no one fails. But we are humans, so there are no guarantees. You can hope that it works out well, but it's rare that it works out really well. Trust is number one. And to have the courage to be in chaos. Have the courage to follow your intuition even if you don't know what it means. Have the courage to say, 'I don't know' for a very long time. It's very hard sometimes to be the director when the actors ask, 'Why?', and you say, 'I don't know. I have a feeling that it's right, but I don't know why.' To accept that you might seem weak. To let go, because it is something that happens. And it's in this 'something that happens' – that it happens. If I don't let go, if I try to figure it out and to get control – then it doesn't happen. Then I get what I already know. What everyone already knows. And then it is just another performance like the ones we already know. It can be very professionally made, but boring as hell. Just another piece.

Mostly, that's what happens, because it is so difficult to make that something extra special. It is very, very difficult to get to that point where you think, 'Yes. That's it.' Sometimes it happens. It is like a ballet dancer. Why do ballet dancers torture themselves so many hours every day? It's because once in a while when they jump they feel as if they are flying. That second when they are sure that they are flying, when they know it's absolutely perfect – that second they want to relive. That's why they torture themselves.

It's the same when you are making a performance; you remember what it's like when it happens and so you try again. It is a drug. You get so high. You feel connected to the whole universe. Everything sounds together. It's so right. It's as Einstein said when someone asked him why his formula was correct: 'Because it is beautiful'. Of course it is.

Trust is not just the condition for you to be able to use your intuition, but also for the actors to be able to use theirs. To liberate it. And not be looking for something specific or wanting to achieve something specific.

That's exactly it. It's not about trying to achieve. It is so far from achievement. That can be very difficult. But it is the same for all artists. If you have been taught to paint, you have to forget that you have been taught to paint. Then you can start painting. If you have been taught to act, you have to forget everything that you have learnt. Then you can start being an actor.

It can be really difficult for me to work with trained actors. Because they can do so much, but one thing is difficult for them: to simply be. What they do is very cleverly done, but it doesn't interest me. What interests me is also what you see in some opera singers that are really brilliant. They go beyond being fantastic singers. They have opened up to the soul, and you can feel that they are singing their own life. They are singing their heartache, or their feeling of being wildly in love. They sing themselves. It is the same with actors, I mean the good ones. But there are very few. It's a very difficult profession, incredibly difficult. You have to dare so much. I respect it enormously.

Problems

What is the biggest problem or difficulty in the rehearsal process? The thing that always get in the way or is hardest to overcome?

It is the problem of not having the courage to be in chaos.

But I want to talk about something else. In Denmark, politics has much too much influence on art. We are placed in a situation that makes it almost impossible to create something other than just a product. To make these extra special things we need time and space. And we are being chased around.

It is a pity that Danish politicians don't ensure that Denmark is able to create great artists. When you look at the great artists around the world there is always the same story behind: they have been given an opportunity, they have had somebody who believed in their talent and gave them freedom and peace. Period. Why did Pina Bausch become Pina Bausch? Because a theatre director said to her, 'Go ahead and work.' Period. None of this, 'Hurry up. You have to produce two performances a year, and if you don't, you don't get any money, and if you don't sell tickets you're out.' People walked out on her performances, they threw tomatoes, and he kept saying, 'Work, just go on working.' It was the same with Peter Brook. For three years he didn't have to produce anything. Three years! Without producing. Three years! Then you become Peter Brook.

I really feel sorry for young people today, because it's hard. You can't be a postman in the morning, take care of disabled people at night, and be creative in between. That's reality. I'm just very sad about that. The production framework makes it difficult. Maybe some people are fast, but I need to be slow. Sometimes you can make something good very fast, it varies a lot, but I need to chew things over. I'm a sort of cow. I need to lie around in a hammock and chew on it, and I need to have periods when I work and then leave it to marinate. And then suddenly I understand what it is I'm doing.

Otherwise it will be controlled by thoughts, and that is a different kind of work. Time pressure is hell. And there is the money... I have been used to work with very little money, so I can say what's good about it, because you become very creative. You find solutions. But it's also a bit of a drag. That you can't make something special or something big.

Dreams

If you could wish for anything in a rehearsal process, and you knew that you would succeed – what would be your utopian or dream process?

Firstly, I would want to have a group of people that I would always work with. I have people that I work with again and again, but I would want to have dancers, and actors, and set designer, and musicians, and composers. A flock, a kind of family that you know you will meet with again and again. You can do things elsewhere, but you get together again and work together again.

And then I would want – something that I usually have, actually – a tiny little period to start with, to open up. Three or four days where you get the feel of the group that you are, and you test what kind of language you want to be working with. A couple of months later: two weeks of intensive improvisation and playing with all parameters. Sound and lights and stage and set design. A few months later another rehearsal period, preferably of two months. All in all a period of roundly three months with gaps in between, where things are allowed to grow.

We do that quite often in [the theatre company] Gruppe 38, and lately I have asked the same thing of The Royal Theatre where I am doing a production this year. They are doing everything they can to give me three work periods. In [the dance company] Aaben Dans we do it that way too. So I have that. One of the things that frustrates me is that everybody is attending to their own business, because everybody is so stressed. It's so complicated to keep your own little shop together, so you hardly have time to meet or to have those periods where you just do something. It's difficult to have a vision, because everything is smothered with worries, financial and political. I am a freelancer, I don't have a business, I only have myself, and that's a choice I made a long long time ago. For good and bad. But at least I'm free. I see how all my friends are suffering under the weight of their jobs. It's a struggle. And when they are going to make a new performance they can hardly breathe just by the thought of it. Because they've had so many other things to do. It's very sad. I deeply respect them for being able to do that.

If you could choose anybody to work with, dead or alive – to do a performance or have in your 'family' – who would that be?

I would have liked to dance for Pina Bausch. Even though I can't dance. That lady would have been able to make me do something. Other than that… There are many. Christopher Marthaler. I would like to sit next to him. He does what I always dream of doing. What he does is always so real. It's always so human, and he always finds a form that is precisely fitting. The way the actors are on stage is so real. And it's so musical and consistent. He's my guru.

I'm quite fond of Heiner Goebbels as well. In another way. Marthaler, because it's so human, and Goebbels, because I'm a visual artist. It's the aesthetics, although I sometimes miss something human. It's funny, because the performance or installation he did two years ago [*Stifter's Things*, 2007] without any people at all, that was human. Pretty extraordinary. There were only machines, no actors, and I was bawling. The way he combined text and lights and images and water and reflection. It became *enormously* sensitive. Emotional. Maybe he is afraid of emotions and only able to create them when there are no people! I don't know if that's true, but it was a very special experience for me. To be crying in front of machines. Very well done.

I want to say something else as well: We have had a debate about whether 'children's theatre' is a word that should be erased. Because children's theatre is not a genre. You can make comedies, you can make tragedies, you can make musicals, you can make opera, you can make ballet or dance performances or cross-over performances, but you cannot make children's performances. Period. It's just theatre that also works for children, where you can bring your children. That's the only difference. Then 70 per cent of the children's theatre that is being made today would not exist. What has been created for children has to do with money. It's an economic way of thinking. Because we buy a lot when it comes to our children, and that's why there are toys and children's this and children's that, because they are commodities. And we shouldn't do that, we shouldn't separate our societies into different groups. We should unite.

And for that reason you should make theatre that people can enjoy together. It's deep, it's life. The other stuff, where you have a child saying, 'Gee, mum, this is fun,' and looks at the mother who is bored to death. The child sees that the mother is bored to death, the child is not stupid. But he wants to please his mother, so he tells her how much fun he is having. He knows what's expected. And we need to stop doing that. But I've worked hard with a lot of my colleagues to change that, and it doesn't get through. Because it's market economy.

You shouldn't make institutional theatre and alternative theatre either. It should be a creative whole. Sometimes you need to be on the road with nothing, sometimes you need to be on the big stages. It should all merge. We shouldn't make these walls.

I was raised in Paris by my parents. They took me to adult theatre from the moment I could sit there without crying. I think I must have been around seven. I was bored stiff. I sat there looking at the lamps and the hats, and then someone out there did something. But it gave me a sense of the theatre. It was a hugely important thing, and I could feel that my parents were elated and happy, and it was nice to go home with them. That was important. It was important to be together. Then it didn't matter one bit that I was bored or not. The important thing was that I felt it did me good. It enters the body. So *down* with children's theatre.

It has happened to me sometimes when I have been touring with Gruppe 38 or Rio Rose abroad. In Denmark it's very difficult, but in other countries you see four generations coming to see the performance. A row with great-grandmother and grandparents, the parents and the children. Then I sit at the back and watch four generations vibrating together. Experiencing the show each at their level. Afterwards all touched, holding each other and kissing and talking. And you know what? Then I think that I have had a good life. Because bringing people together is what theatre is. It's a ritual. It's like the church. You make something that has been healed. And people are humans and feel the whole universe. Great words. Great vision.

The best thing I've done for the past few years has been *You Me Us* [2008] for Aaben Dans, which is for babies. It gives me that joy. They are tiny babies and everything is done on the level of the senses. And then their parents. And they melt into each other completely. Symbiosis and calm. It works. It does them good.

Interview: Barbara Simonsen

Catherine Poher (FR/DK)
Catherine Poher (born 1953) is a director and visual artist based in Copenhagen. She has directed performances at Theatre Rio Rose, 'Teatret' with Hans Rønne and at the Royal Danish Theatre, among others. Her work is mainly driven by a wish to create theatre for children and adults alike. Her performances are characterized by a special focus on the spontaneous, the sensual and the simple, speaking to audiences of all ages.

Select works
Den komiske Tragedie (1993)
Ta' Ti Ting (2002)
Du må være en engel Hans Christian (2005)
HANe og HUNd (2014)

Website
www.catherinepoher.dk

Notes

1 See Chapter 5, pages 71–80.

2 *La Tragédie Comique* (1988) by La Fabrique Imaginaire, a Belgian company led by Yves Hunstad and Eve Bonfanti. An interview with Hunstad and Bonfanti from 2008 is part of the Rehearsal Matters collection at www.rehearsalmatters.org

17

Berit Stumpf and Sean Patten

Why

Why did you choose to work with theatre or performance?

Sean: I think… Because it's live. Although we are very interested in film, in video, in TV, and we are always working with video cameras, we really treasure the uniqueness of the live experience. This thing that… it can only happen once, even if you're touring a production it's different every night, and it's different every day with each audience there. It's a very special, unique situation, which is still very valuable and important today.

Berit: Yes, I would also say that mostly in our work we are actually trying to strengthen this live character, through working with new elements that strengthen the potential of the here and now, the moment-like. Through working with risk factors that can change the product completely every night.

How

Can you give a short description of your creative process from the first idea to the final product?

Berit: Sure, the work and the product are almost inseparable for us. In the work processes we always try to develop a set-up or create a situation which then at some point becomes a performance. During the process we try to create or to find the structure, within which we can improvise and try out. That means, for example, walking in the streets with cameras to find the framework that will narrow it down even further. Finding rules for playing, and trying out, and improvising. And so process and product are very close and very strongly connected.

Sean: Yeah, it's funny, I think over the years – we've been going fourteen years now – we have developed quite our own way of making work. We sometimes have students or people come to observe it, and they will experience very different things. Sometimes we'll spend a week where it's just talking about the idea. Sometimes they'll experience that we are doing lots and lots of stuff. The way it works is often that you have an idea and then you write about it and by the time you actually come to get round to doing it, one or two years later, things have moved on. So the first stage is to formalize the idea, and bring it up to speed and check that the idea is still interesting and appropriate. The idea is often based around a site or a situation. For example the idea to make a performance piece in a hotel through the night. Or the idea to make a film where people walk onto the streets with synchronized cameras. Ideas are often an audience-performer set up situation at the site and we'll try very early on in the process to test that idea in a very basic way.

How do you do that?

Berit: Usually we try to create as exactly as possible the framework that belongs to the idea. Naturally that is difficult sometimes. When we say that we would really like to develop something during a night in a hotel, there comes the utopian element, because it's next to impossible to get a hotel for a month where we can try out for real this situation that we have thought of. So we try to find something that comes as close as possible. Maybe we'll start to rehearse in a flat, where all the performers are in separate rooms, and because there are only a few rooms you have to arrange it so that there are only two performers at a time. In *Room Service* [2003], the project that I'm talking about here, we performers are alone in each hotel room for one night and have to occupy and entertain ourselves. In each room there is a camera and a telephone that connect you to the outer world, and the audience is in the conference room of the hotel, and you try to establish contact with the audience. The subtitle is 'Help me make it through the night', so it's about getting through a sleepless night together. And yes, in this case we tried to find a flat with as many rooms as possible. We used the kitchen as a mini-command centre or conference room where the technicians would sit, but also the external eyes that we always take turns to be within our team. That is very important to us, since we work as a collective and therefore the external eye is a function that we change around and not a permanent person. We also tried establishing a camera connection to the rooms and gave each performer a certain amount of time there – in the beginning we said half an hour and it seemed like an eternity – to try to build something, and play and improvise within this framework that we keep enlarging and supplying with rules.

What rules might that be?

Sean: For example, you are not allowed to stop. If you get completely stuck in an improvisation you are not allowed to say it's over. We're going to run this for sixty minutes and getting stuck is part of the process. Or a completely different thing: when you are talking to the camera you can only use the past tense – or you mustn't speak at all. So always finding out rules. And then the rehearsals move on, once we've established this set-up – this example of *Room Service* that Berit has just given – and with other shows, what the constraints are or what the situation is. Then we'll alternate between having sessions where we try and develop material, and we don't necessarily know what kind of structure or plan it's going into – and maybe another team of people will sit down and think about the material we've developed in the last few weeks and try to think, how could this be structured in some way. Then we'll try and roughly talk through a structure. This bit, this bit, going in to this bit, this bit… Kind of walk through it and then try it. So it's alternating between trying to work on a structure, a vision for the whole thing, and having some free play where you can throw up new stuff, where you don't care where it's going.

I think the crucial thing is with us as a collective that we're always sort of switching hats. So, sometimes I'll come in to rehearsal and I'll just be a performer. Maybe I've got a hangover or I'm not feeling too well and I'll just say to the others, 'Look, just tell me what to do, I'm here to realize your idea.' Sometimes someone will come in, they will have had a hot bath the night before, with a brainwave, and they'll say, 'I've got a brainwave! Let's do this.' And then because we always have more people – for example in this project we here in Aarhus with, *Super Night Shot* [2003] – there's now nine people who could perform it, but we only need four roles. So in the rehearsal process two or three people will watch, four people will do, and then the next night we'll swap it round.

Berit: It's a bit like a football team, perhaps. Where there is also always someone on the bench, but in this case with a purpose, because being on the outside is part of the process. It's quite important for all of us that we sometimes take this distance and really look at what we are producing from the outside, and of course you see things differently. Especially because we work so much with media, very often, as with *Room Service*, you have no idea at all of the overall picture while you're making and rehearsing it. You are alone in your own world and have lost the overview, so you get that back and you also see things with the others where maybe you have an idea that you can develop further. The material that we develop is accessible to everyone; there is no such thing as individual authorship or saying, this is my baby and I'll be the only one to use it. All the material goes into the pool and belongs to everyone. This constant shifting between within and without – being in it and looking at it – is completely essential, I think, for our entire process.

Sean: Like a small element of an idea. You can sort of trace its evolution through the process. Maybe one day I'll put on a rabbit mask and do a silly dance and it won't actually be that good. But maybe the next day someone else will think, alright, that was interesting, maybe I'll wear it and do it in a different way. So every idea that gets put into the thing belongs to the project, belongs to the group. And then it gets used, copied, played for laughs, played seriously. Everything that you do in rehearsal belongs to the group and its material.

About the collective decisions: What do you do if you have tried something out and two of the group think it's brilliant while three others think that it's terrible?

Berit: Mostly we try to stay with it and maybe get it somewhere where the others can bring something to it that they can identify with. Because we can't put anything on stage that we can't all really identify with, so it has to be found. And mostly this consensus can be found. It's also a question of time.

Sean; It's also the way you approach it. Obviously, that situation you described is a very confrontational one. So then, the thing we would do is to say, 'Okay, these three people who hate this…'

Berit: '… you take over.'

Sean: 'You know what we are trying to do, roughly – you give it a try. Do it your way and show us something.' Because just talking against something is not going to bring it further. We try to move through a confrontational blockage like this by people doing something so they can show us the way. Because anyone can sit here and say, 'It should be like this, it should be like that – blah, blah, blah.' Of course, talking is part of the process, but until we can actually see something playing on stage or behind the camera it can't move forward.

Berit: And another thing is that we try to develop paths or parts. We don't develop roles as such, but certain paths through the piece or certain parts, and these are filled out in a very individual way. When I see how Sarah [Thom] is doing a particular part then I know that I will be doing it quite differently, and of course that gives you a certain tolerance towards it, because you can accept that Sarah does it the way she does and I will do it in another way. For sure there are things that I do that Sarah would never do, but that's okay, she will do it like this then. And within this larger structure that stays the same, things are filled out individually, and obviously everyone can put their own preferences, strengths and weaknesses into it.

Sean: An example is *Room Service*, this project which happens in a hotel. In some ways, it's a journey from isolation – the four performers completely on their own, the audience witnessing them – to some brief moments of connection between the audience and performers. Berit and Sarah both play a role where at a certain point we all agree there has to be what we call a close encounter between a performer and an audience member. This is our basic path. The performer has to fulfill this. Berit's way is often to call somebody up and they dance together in their room silently in the dark.

Berit: And it's building up a fantasy together that they play someone from my past or whatever…

Sean: Sarah's way is to approach it from a completely different way with a lot of humour, and to say, 'I'd like to have a relationship in my room. Not the beginning, not the end, but just the middle. And then somebody comes to the room and sometimes they just eat crisps and watch TV. They've both fulfilled the path of finding a connection, which is sort of touching, but also humorous. But they've both done it in their own way.

How do you avoid always falling into the usual roles in your collaboration?

Berit: I think very often you know somehow that certain people are good at making a dramaturgy or a structure at a certain point. Also some people love that and others might hate it. Others prefer to act and to proceed more intuitively. And we know that about each other, of course, so often it's similar or the same people, but not always. Also you know that these people will bring it in this or that direction, and in that sense it's good that two other people, who work in a different way and much more intuitively, also take on the task of making the structure. Very often it goes through several pairs of hands before it is done the way we want it. Therefore you can't just say that this person always does this and that's how it's made; often there is a first impulse that is then passed on. And I think that is very characteristic of what we… It's a bit like these paintings where you paint something and pass it on and somebody else paints on it. It's very characteristic about our process that things often change hands. And so they always carry more than one handwriting.

The essential

What is the ideal rehearsal process like? Is there a connection between the rehearsal process and the final product? In short, super rehearsal process equals super product?

Berit: I would say, generally yes, but not always. There are also cases where you have had a unbelievable, fantastic, relaxed rehearsal process and somehow you don't get any further or it doesn't really fall into place. It's not always identical. But in general it is, I guess. Time is always important – to have a large time frame and not so much pressure. That's why we often choose to work in several phases, to get a distance to one phase before entering into another, and then of course it gets more intense as the project comes along.

Sean: Yes, for example, recently we've been lucky enough to get enough funding to work for sort of fourteen weeks on a project, but we like to spread it out over nine months. So we have like a first couple of weeks and then we'll do a month where we are touring or doing another project, then we will come back. So always going into it and then doing something else to get a break, and then a final six-week push.

I think the most crucial thing is that the concept, or this basic idea or situation is good. And holds water. Because on paper everything can sound great, and then the crucial thing is in the first part of rehearsing, testing. Does this actually work in reality? With some projects, it's proven to work, and then none of these big questions about, 'Why we are doing it? What is it for? Could it be twenty-four hours? Could it be thirty minutes? Shouldn't we better do it in a bus with old ladies?' or whatever – none of these fundamental questions come up. Everyone is happy with the concept, and it's just a question of fulfilling its potential. Then it goes well.

Sometimes you get a project where the idea sounds great on paper, but it becomes pretty soon clear that as a performance or as an experience it's fundamentally flawed and then you have to start again and that's very difficult.

Berit: We've already mentioned the rules that we use to define our rehearsal processes and that we always try to find, because they are very important to us. We try to frame the improvisations and find the rules that will define the play and make it clearer. To find this mixture of freedom and form. It's always ideal when this framework or set-up, and partly the rules as well, come easily. In *Room Service* it's somehow very clear that the set-up demands certain rules. You can't hear each other between the rooms; you're alone, and it's an entire night. It's clearly a durational performance. You don't have to construct all these things from scratch, because they are really given within the parameters of the framework that is already in itself conceptual. Then you have to refine it, of course. But overall, it's self-explanatory. And those are the strongest starting points, where so much is given and found. On the other hand, when we feel that the framework is arbitrary, and you think, yes, it could last two hours or four, what should decide it, is the limit when people get bored or… When all these factors come from the basic idea that is of course ideal.

When is your collaboration ideal?

Sean: When everybody is not too tired, and not too busy, and had a good holiday.

Berit: What's ideal is when you are moving on a wave. When there are no big misunderstandings. It happens automatically that someone pulls more in one direction and someone else in another, and sometimes things can partially separate. Someone is working more on the thread and someone else is trying to take things to where he wants them. We always try to let every idea be a possibility and not rule out anything beforehand. Because we know – and that's why we have worked together for so long – that we trust each other in this field, even if you don't understand at all what the other one is talking about or where he might want to go with it. We'll say, 'Okay, let's try it,' and only then you might see something that you think has potential. So to start with, there is no censure, everything can be tried out. We're very willing to give everyone the possibility to try something out. We know that we can't judge it until it's been tried. You have to test the reality of it, before you can reject it.

Sean: I think we are aware that particularly in a group there can be a tendency to talk. To talk about it and to talk each other into corners or to talk ideas in and out of existence. Now that we have been together for some time we are aware of that, so we are always trying to get to the stage where an idea can move from a piece of paper or words into something you can actually see. And so this is our effort to try and get things in reality, even if it's very rough. That they can be worked on.

Berit: During rehearsals we are often a very large team, because we work with a lot of guests, so what we'll do very often is separate into small groups for a while. We'll say, 'For the next two hours I'll be working with participation,' and someone else says, 'I have to try out this thing with the camera.' Or someone might have an idea about the structure. And then you say, 'Okay, who feels close to whom?' or 'Who can begin with this idea?' And so you go together into small teams without everyone having to work on it beforehand or having to have their own idea about it. We divide and then we come together and present it practically, a small set-up or try-out or something. And of course that brings us a step further: the others can see how it fits in and you can have a clear discussion or evaluation of it. We do this very often, dividing and coming together and showing, and from that something new emerges and is connected.

Problems

What problems seem impossible to solve, and what problems don't you want to experience ever again?

Berit: Well, that's a very harsh way of putting it. We had one rehearsal process that was really very, very hard for me, where we didn't really know what we were doing right up to the end. That was somehow at the limit where you felt that no one knew what we were actually working on, and a lot of factors were complete question marks more or less until the opening. We worked more on it after that and I think that reconciled us to the product, at least. It was one of the first set-ups where we worked very strongly with audience participation and that in itself made it very difficult, of course, because we wanted very early on, conceptually as well, for the audience to be the actual main character of the project. It all took place in a large tent that was set up in the theatre, and it was all about creating a kind of ceremony that would fit to our modern, secularized world. Defining a sort of community together with the audience, creating a new world somehow. Anyway, we sat there five or six people together at a time, and of course we didn't have the whole audience that was the main part of the project. So we kept beating around the bush, talking it to death, and didn't know how to grasp the whole thing or to try it out. How can you try something out that is really by definition a happening?

But then we started making semi-public try-outs with invited audiences, and that was actually something that we took with us in other projects, also when the audience is less directly involved, because it really brings us further. Where you engage very early on with the audience and set up the situation. We haven't done it often enough, though, despite the fact that these try-outs have always been good and important; we should have done it even more. So that the final jump into the opening had been less of a jump into cold water, in front of an audience that is the worst kind for that, namely critics and journalists, or producers who prefer to sit in the corner and watch from the outside, judging and seeing if they want to buy it or not. And they are not to be compared with our nice try-out audiences that consist of friends and acquaintances. But anyway, it was a very difficult process where we were pushed to our limits. And within the process there was another thing, that inside the group there was a lot of tension about the work, that people weren't going in the same direction anymore, and it wasn't a coincidence that directly afterwards two people left the group because they wanted to focus on their video work. It was a difficult phase and a difficult project for us.

Sean: I always think they're awful. Every rehearsal process there comes a point where I'm so depressed. I hate everybody. I want to leave the group. It's always awful – at a certain point.

Why?

Sean: Because there's a lot of pressure. You put a lot of pressure on yourself, because you want it to be good. You want to go on with the work, and of course, a lot depends on the success of the project. And then there comes a point about two thirds of the way through where you realize, 'All of the dreams I once had about this project, now there is not enough time to realize them.' It's a critical point, a journey between idealism and dreaming and being pragmatic and working on the details. At this point, it's very hard because you have to let go of a lot of stuff. You have to get realistic and make the best out of what you have. And this is very difficult to deal with emotionally, to let go of that and move on to the next phase. It always makes me very ill and depressed.

Berit: But Sean has rather a short-term memory about this and always thinks that the rehearsal process he is in is the worst there has ever been, and then you have to remind him that to be honest we were in exactly the same spot at the same time in the last project.

Sean: Well, ultimately, I'm still here because it's worth it. Most of the time. The products I'm very happy with. When we tour them and show them to people it's mostly fulfilling and rewarding, and it's worth the trauma, otherwise I wouldn't still be doing it. But there is this point where you have to say goodbye to a lot of stuff.

Berit: I really think it's true that two thirds into the time frame there is often a critical phase, because you have to say goodbye to all these possibilities that are there in the beginning. It's no longer like in the beginning when you can say, anything goes and tomorrow we can try out something completely new. At some point there is a phase where you say stop, we have tried out enough and now we have to find something in the material that we have developed. We are not so rigorous that we say that from now on there can be no new ideas at all, but overall you know that now you have to accept what has been developed so far and ask, 'What is this? What can we make of this?' That can be frustrating, if you feel that you haven't attained what you wanted, or you have to face reality.

Sean: I think it must be terrible – very difficult to work as a producer or technical director for us. Because we hate this point where we have to make the clear decisions. Of course they are under pressure to know, look, is it in a shop or in a theatre? One camera or none? Of course, these questions have to be answered, but we always like to leave it as late as possible to make us find things.

How can you improve the process so that you avoid this frustration?

Berit: I always have the feeling that you sometimes set these traps for yourself. I mean, we often think out a very complicated technical set-up. And then you have to accept the reality of the technique. That's really our own bed we've made and we have to lie in it. Therefore, I also feel that we can't make anyone else responsible for changing it except ourselves. We often take the consequence and say, 'Next time no cameras,' but then mostly we don't do it, because our love and fascination for the technical is just too great, and of course that's what makes it all possible. So we're not ready to really say, now we'll go puristically back to having nothing on stage, because we work so much with materials and technique. I don't know how you could avoid this phase; I have the feeling that it's somehow part of the whole, it's like a birth, and the hard labour is part of it. Sean, what do you think?

Sean: Yeah. It‘s our own fault.

Dreams

What would you like to try out, if anything was possible?

Berit: First of all, I think it would be interesting to take away the pressure, and to be able to change the time frame according to your wishes and ideas.

Sean: We say it's ready when it's ready…

Berit: Yes. So you have no kind of outside-determined calendar of the whole thing.

Sean: Although, would we ever say it's ready?

Berit: Good question. Maybe… I don't know. I would be interested to say – because we have been in situations where it was obvious that the idea came very late, and it would have been great to say, 'Okay, now we want another four weeks.' And to really get at home with it.

Sean: Yes. That‘s the main factor. Time. It always creeps up on you, and you never feel that you have enough time. But I wonder, even if you had all the time in the world, if it might run out of steam. I don't know, but that would definitely be high on the utopia list.

Berit: And another very concrete situation for us: it would of course be ideal if you could work from the beginning in the situation that you have imagined. That you could create it immediately. For example work in a hotel.

Sean: Or a hospital, then we can work in a hospital and not in a theatre pretending to be a hospital.

Berit: Because from the outset you have to simply cancel a lot of ideas, because you know that it's not realistic, you won't have time for it, and if you do, it will be very late. In spite of that, we often throw ourselves into something like that, like with the hotel, and somehow we make it work. You try to work for a long time in a situation that is as close as possible to the real one, but naturally it's not the same. And the real conditions would create a totally different starting point.

Do you ever feel like working in a different way, for example not in a collective, but with a director?

Sean: I don't want to be a director. Really. I think it must be quite lonely at the top.

We often have ideas where we want hundreds of extras. And horses, and dancing dogs, and fireworks, and boats… So it would be great, particularly people. We always have ideas where we need three hundred children on white horses riding past, and it would be great to be able to do something like that. Now I'm thinking it would just be like the Beijing Olympic opening…

Berit: Yeah, that's the question…

Sean: But it would be great to try it. I'd love to try one of those Olympic opening ceremonies. I think that would be really funny.

Berit: It would be an organizational nightmare.

Sean: Yes, but you'd have the team. You'd have the people, wouldn't you? I'd really love to know what you can do if you have five hundred people.

Berit: But then they all want to know from *you* what they should do at what time.

Sean: Yeah… Because we are working with cameras, a lot of our process is similar to the process of making a film. But we don't have film budgets. And we realize every time that there is a reason why, when you go to the cinema, it takes ten minutes just for the credits to roll by, why films need hundreds of people, every one with a little job. Of course, this is what's good about our aesthetic, that we do all do it ourselves with cheap little cameras and one-man film teams. But sometimes it would be great to really realize a vision with a big crew and a big team of extras.

Berit: I think I want the technique to be further, to be where our heads are. To not always have the limits of, 'Oh no, you can't have that live link'.

Sean: Yeah. Live, ultra-high definition video links. *Like* we've been promised since the 1960s.

Berit: They're still not really working.

Sean: They don't work. We have a lot of ideas, which are based on this thing, but technology is nowhere near there.

Interview: Isabelle Reynaud

Berit Stumpf (DE) and Sean Patten (UK)
Berit Stumpf (born 1969) and Sean Patten (born 1971) are co-founding members of the international performers' collective Gob Squad, formed in 1994. Gob Squad makes performances, videos, installations and happenings, mixing theatre, performance, film and real life. The group tours worldwide with their works.

Select works
House (1994)
The Great Outdoors (2001)
Room Service (Help Me Make It Through the Night) (2003)
War and Peace (2016)

Website
www.gobsquad.com

18

Wayn Traub

Why

Why did you choose to work with theatre or how did you end up in theatre?

Originally, I took an education in film. But I arrived at that through – since my childhood – a sort of love for the stage. I did classical ballet, and in school I was always doing little theatre pieces with the boys from my class. So I had a sort of attraction to theatre, but the vision that I had of what I wanted to do on stage was much more cinematographic. Because I also had a great love of the cinema, and my father worked as cameraman and editor. And I was influenced by that already at a very early age. I made my own little films and montages from the age of twelve. Little clips with music and songs.

So it was clear that I wanted to do a mix of the two. When I had finished my film education I didn't feel ready to start making films, and I went on to study art history at the university for four years. And there I specialized in theatre, that's where it started to interest me, especially theatre with an element of ritual. Not just a theatre that narrated stories, but that had a ritual significance. And that's where I really chose to do theatre over other things. Even though I still believe that I am going to make films, I realized that I have to pass through theatre. Especially because of this ritual element that I don't find easy to create with film, because there isn't this presence between you and the audience, and I missed that somehow.

So that's why I started doing theatre, and from the beginning it was a very personal form of theatre, and with a lot of cinematographic elements. There you have the mix: I do pieces where you have film at the same time as you have the actors on stage, and also the way in which I make my actors play on stage, and the accompanying music, always gives an impression of cinema. So that's it, I guess.

How

Can you describe you work process from idea to final product?

First of all, I never work with existing things. I believe that theatre, or any art form… I do what I feel I have to. I make coats of arms [*points around the room*], they are all over the place, I take photos, I make films, clips: and I also make theatre. The only thing that interests me is to create. I think that to create is to call oneself into question. When you create, you look at yourself in the mirror. I think the main reason that I do things is that I want to look at myself in the mirror. To grow richer personally, spiritually and so on. And in the end to accept what it is one has to do on this earth.

So for me, any use of an element from somebody else feels like a kind of betrayal to myself. And like an easy option. I don't like to watch theatre pieces where they use a text by Shakespeare or another person, or even music by somebody else, something that hasn't been written especially for this project, because I think it's too easy. What I've never understood is why in music in general we only accept new creations as true artistic creations, and if a group only plays songs by others, for example The Beatles, we don't take them seriously, because they are only redoing what has been done a thousand times – whereas in theatre the greatest directors are those who do Shakespeare. That I don't understand. I never have. To me a creation has to be a true creation.

That's why everything I do is, from A to Z, created especially for this. The music is created for the performance, the text is created for the performance, the costumes, the idea, the concept, the scenario; everything is original.

And when I said that I create theatre as a kind of mirror it's because I really believe that the reason for making art – certainly for me – is that I want above all to make something that is completely personal. I think the more personal it is the more universal it becomes. Artists like Brel or Kubrick were super personal, they simply expressed what they believed, what they felt, and what they wanted to narrate and share with people, and because of that everybody recognized themselves in it.

I have really chosen to be as honest as possible in what I have done. I never look for a theme to write about. I don't look for what I want to do next year. I often work on three or four projects at the same time. I work with boxes. When I think that a project is really coming into existence I make a box for it, and I put all the ideas into it. The box that fills up the fastest is the one that is asking to be realized. That's why I made *Maria-Dolores* [2002] first and then *Jean-Baptiste* [2006], and it took four years before making *Maria-Magdalene* [2009] – which I'm doing now – because the ideas weren't ready for this performance, so I did other things that were ready.

How do I work? I always work – or I have for thirteen years – with books, little black notebooks. It's what I do from morning till night. I have about a hundred of these little books. And when I find a photograph that I like in a magazine, for example, I keep it and I stick it in the book. Then I start drawing next to it the character that I want to play, thinking it could be something like that. I draw constantly, I find articles, I write in it. In a book like this there are several projects at the same time, and when I've found something I make a copy of it and put it in the box.

That's the base. After that, when I know more clearly the feeling of the show, I know it will be something in this direction, the first thing I do is to work on the music. Which is strange, normally you start by writing the scenario and then you work on the music, when everything has been filmed, or even at the last moment, people will put music here and there to fill out the gaps. Something that I hate – I don't like to watch shows where they put a little Mozart here and a little Beethoven there. I think that the music is the emotional base of something. I work for four, five, six months only on the music. Getting the feeling of what is the potential atmosphere of this performance. Often we have thirty to forty drafts of music, of songs, and from these we choose seven or eight. Based on these songs, I start to write the final scenario.

The songs are written in a collaboration between me and the composer. For *Maria-Dolores* and *Jean-Baptiste* it was Wim de Wilde, a Flemish composer, and for two years now I have been working with Jaan Hellkvist. We work together very intensively; the music is created by him, and I sing to it, that is my part of the creation. So it goes back and forth, and it's a real collaboration.

So once the music is ready, I'll write the final scenario. It's about 70 per cent written, it's never 100 per cent finished, but it's a good material to work on. And my work method is that I start by filming the scenario, that takes two months. Then I begin the montage – that's what I'm doing right now with this performance [*Maria-Magdalene*] – and that takes another two months. Finally, I will do one month of rehearsals on stage. But the rehearsals will take place at the same time as the montage, things overlap, even though I'm doing the montage I will be going to film something today etc. As I work in small teams I can change quickly, and when I see that there is something missing in the montage we can go filming again. It happens very organically. It's not like on a big stage where you have to put something on and then you can't move it around. That's not how I work.

So, if you count all the months, I work on a project for one year before the opening. After having done the concept. Naturally, including that it takes longer. I worked on *Maria-Dolores* for a year and a half, on *Jean-Baptiste* for a year and a half, and on this one, *Maria-Magdalene*, I will have worked for three years, including the concept, the ideas, the work.

In the beginning I told you that I work primarily with myself in order to be as universal as possible. It's what I've always believed in; I work for the 'I, you, they', and that's sort of my credo. First of all, I want to be in harmony with myself, and I believe quite simply that if you are, it makes you ready to be with the 'you', the people around you, the people that you work with every day, the family. I think it's a long stage to go. It's a huge amount of work, because you have to be just as honest with them, you have to be kind to them too, and it's a lot of work. And thirdly, there is always the true purpose of art or an artist, to reach the 'they'. To touch, to be honest and good, to caress and to strike at the same time the people that you don't know, the people who come to see the performance, and the people who come after. All the great artists continue to live through the great quality of their work that continues to touch people. Jacques Brel is dead, but he still touches us. That's the 'they'. And I think the complete artist will reach people, in the long term, not in the short term with a fast little success and then you're forgotten. So overall, those are the lines along which I work.

How do you choose your performers?

That depends. There aren't really any rules. I meet people and am attracted to them, and often the encounter with an actress or a person is the reason for writing a character around this person. It happens very rarely that I write a character first and then look for an actor who can play the role. Very often I have met someone that I find so amusing and special that he or she inspires me to write something about him or her. In the performance that I'm doing now most of the people, the amateurs and the professionals… I gave some workshops in China a year ago, and I saw the most incredible female dancers. I had no intention as such of working with them, but I thought they were so good that I started writing about them. There is a Colombian actor, Omar Porras, who has a theatre called Teatro Malandro, a superb theatre and an amazing actor. For years I have dreamt of writing something for him, I had ideas for him, I pictured him performing things. And now he acts in the film as well. There is a pop singer called Gabriel Rios that I think has a fantastic personality. I happened to see him play and I liked him so much that I started writing a character for him. Of course, these characters are not just written about them, they also come through me, because I write what I want to communicate through them. But that is my main source of inspiration. I am very rarely inspired by nothing or by an image of someone; I want to meet a real person. Once in Holland there was a girl who came to speak to me after a performance, a Dutch girl, and she had red hair. And at that moment, when I saw her, while I was speaking to her, I said to myself, I have to write something about this red girl. Now she is in the film. There is an equal number of amateurs and professionals. I guess that's how it is.

Do you co-create with your team, or are you the primary creative force?

Two years ago I was working with a group of actors, and I wanted to give them the possibility of creating something together with me, to give much more input. But it didn't work. It wasn't because of them, it was because of me – I think I have a universe that is very finished, and in which I know very precisely what I want to tell. And as I have said, I can't perform a piece by someone else, I can't realize someone else's scenes, what they want to realize. What they want to do they have to do themselves.

I think I'm best at inspiring people. I bring a concept that is very clear, ideas that are very clear. There are artists who need to be given a world and who are best at creating within that. I have always worked better with these artists, who need a little surplus from someone else, who don't write themselves, but when someone comes and gives them the motor, they start to write and create miracles. I think the majority of the people that I work with are like this. They need my inspiration to be able to create. And very often they create things that I couldn't. In a certain area they are much better than me, and the combination between us works well. The collaboration that I'm having now with the composer is of this kind, and also with another composer that I've worked with. It worked very well because of that. With some of the actors it's the same. Simonne Moesen, who also acts in this film, and who acted in *Marie-Dolores*, is someone who is very creative, has many ideas, and who writes very well, and she has her own ideas as well, I think – but I can see that she works very well when I give her a lot of elements. Much faster. When we discuss and explore too much together, it doesn't really work, and I feel that with a lot of people. It's good to bring a concept that is very clear. And that's how I work with people. An inspirer [*laughs*].

The essential

What is in your experience the essential condition for a rehearsal process to succeed?

I think that what I've noticed over the years is that the idea with which you begin has to be very strong. I've noticed that when I come to rehearsals with an idea that I am not sure about, that hasn't been made sufficiently strong in advance, very often it doesn't get any better. Whereas a very good idea becomes even better. Because the person who is going to perform it or do it is so inspired that he will be able to use all his force to make it even better. And also, automatically, it creates a much stronger atmosphere somehow. It's like cooking: the better vegetables, fruit and ingredients you use, the better the meal will be. I think there have been periods in my life – I think everybody has it in them, a kind of laziness – where you think you're a genius and that you always come up with a good idea. I've really had to put that aside. I try to prepare my ideas until they are very strong, and to wait quite a long time before presenting them. That's what I do with the notebooks; I work for a very long time before I set things in motion. Looking at all the stages that I've passed through to create the costumes for my new characters before actually making them, it's really impressive. Just this week we were scanning all the drawings of the nuns – there are nuns in the film, Asian nuns – and when you look at all the drawings… I've been through three different costume designers, and it really wasn't until the last moment that we found the right costume. Sometimes it's very quick, and sometimes it takes time, and I've really learned that if it's not there, you don't do it. If the idea isn't strong enough you'll burn your fingers. I don't do that anymore.

So for me things succeed if… Frankly, if the idea is strong enough, in my experience you always succeed. Some days are better than others, of course, but things seem to proceed quickly. I've also learned that in everything you do you have to work with people who are really excellent. I don't think you will reach this kind of level… You need some kind of education in what you do. I think that when someone is thirty years old he is formed and he does what he is capable of. So I always try to work with the best – people who are very strong within their field – and I've noticed that every time you work with people of that calibre the result is five times better than the original idea. So I think the second element, after the element of having a good base, a good idea, is the people around you, who have to be very good. And who need to at least have the level of a professional or a master.

The third level is the external eye. Even with the best people you become blind to the result. It's strange, it's frightening; it's because you start to love what you have made, and you don't notice the flaws anymore. That's when an idiot comes in and destroys the whole atmosphere that you've created so nicely. And it's very necessary. That someone says, 'Why, it looks like a smurf, this thing that you've made,' and you go, 'Huh? A smurf? My God, it is a smurf!' You don't see the faults anymore. Sometimes, though, it confirms exactly what you want to do, and that's why the external eye is extremely important. I've even noticed that when you invite someone from the outside, several persons, it is as if the energy of someone else transforms you at that moment. I've watched rehearsals with my actors, where I have invited three or four people, sat down next to them, and I could see for myself that it wasn't good. Even though I had already watched it five or six times and found it good. I watch it in exactly the same way, but I absorb the energy from the others, and I realize that it's not good. Regardless of the fact that these people say afterwards that it's brilliant, you still have the feeling that it's not that good. It's not a question of being unsure of yourself, it's because you really feel it at that moment. I've learned a lot from these experiences where I've invited people. I used to be afraid of that and avoided it, but now I do it, against my own inclination, I invite people. It's not pleasant [*smiles*].

Those are the three stages, I think, that give me a successful rehearsal and creation period. Afterwards, the audience comes, and I'm totally indifferent to what the audience thinks about my work. I'm very honest, I don't do things to entertain people, but I know that it touches them if it's made honestly. So if it's a great success or people think it's fantastic, that doesn't touch me any more than if someone hates it or thinks it's crap. To me, the most important thing is the creation in itself, and after that it lives its own life. And if it's a success you have a lot of friends, if it's not a success you have fewer friends [*laughs*]. Well. You just have to move on and develop what you do.

The people who come to watch rehearsals, are they just ordinary people, friends, or dramaturgs?

It's very often a mix. It's people who: 1) know my work well, 2) don't know anything, have never seen anything, and 3) people who know me and who are very critical. Who will always be honest with me. Those are the three types of people that I will invite to watch a performance. I listen to what is said, and at the same time I don't take into account anything that they say. In neither case: there are those who think it's really good and don't want me to change anything, and those who don't like it at all and want to change everything. I've noticed that at that moment you know very well what you have to do. You can sense where the fault is. People around you exaggerate in the direction of too much or too little, but you have to stay very clear yourself. You know where it should go. This is true, this isn't true. Yesterday I had three drawings that I showed to my brother and I asked him, 'Which one is the best?' And he said the one that I thought was the worst of them, absolutely the worst. 'That one is the best.' Now I could doubt myself, but I don't. He has his reasons, he doesn't know the project and he doesn't know how I see it. So I said, no no, I'm going to stay on track. That happens too.

Which rehearsal process has been the most successful one in your career and why?

It's strange, *Maria-Dolores* has undoubtedly been my greatest success so far. And it's the piece that has given me least satisfaction. I've always felt bad about the piece, I've always thought that it wasn't finished, and there has always been technical problems. Every time I've performed it, I've been afraid that things wouldn't work, that the video would stop, people would fall over… So *Maria-Dolores* was not my best experience.

I once did a performance with elderly people in Chalon-sur-Saône [France]. I worked with them for two weeks, and I had almost nothing prepared beforehand, but I knew one thing: that I wanted to make them die constantly on stage. They were all over the age of seventy. And there was such a human warmth; it was so beautiful to do it with them and my most beautiful experience in theatre. We only played it twice. The idea was that they came on stage one by one and died in one way or another. It was the only thing that we did. And then there was the Virgin Mary, played by my girlfriend at the time, Marie [Lecomte], who came and raised them from the dead. She did a little prayer and they got up: 'Ah, I've been brought back' [*laughs*]. It was so funny, and the whole team of elderly people were so sweet that I remember it as one of the most beautiful experiences I've had in theatre.

The other thing is that this year, after two difficult years of working only with theatrical experiments that were very heavy for me I've rediscovered the joy of working with the people who also worked with me during the difficult period, and who didn't abandon me because of it. Who continued after all. And that for me is the most beautiful experience, humanly and professionally, that I have had. To have people around me who didn't give up on me, who continued to work with the same enthusiasm – and all for an idea that's crazy, it's theatre. I find that very impressive. They are people with children, for example, they take a risk in doing this, but they still do it. I'm very grateful. It makes me very happy. It's been such a pleasure for me to do all this filming, and I have a beautiful team around me, which is what gives me the greatest satisfaction. People around me who keep working and who do it well.

Problems

Artistically speaking, it's really difficult for me to be satisfied with my work. I'm never happy with it, I keep thinking it should have been better, I'm always left with an emptiness. But maybe that is also the reason why I continue. Maybe if one day I feel satisfied I won't have the energy to do it again. It's very dual, at the same time happy and not happy; I get a new project going and at the same time I'm never happy with what I do. So for the artistic result I can never say that this or this project satisfied me. I've always gotten more satisfaction from the collaboration with people. Or from the moment of creation rather than the result. I don't enjoy applause at all, for example. I've even decided not to go on for the applause anymore. It bothers me, we're like clowns looking for the audience's applause. I don't make theatre for the sake of the applause, not even primarily for the audience. So I don't want to do that anymore. It makes me feel as if I am betraying myself. As if I come on stage because I need the applause. In the coming performance I'm the only performer. I will be alone on stage for an hour and a half, and I think that's enough! I've done what I was supposed to and I don't want to be the little monkey who comes in at the end to ask for a sort of recognition from the audience. I think people have to work it out on their own. If it's a good piece, it has enough value for them to take home. Yes, I have a strange sort of relationship with the artistic result.

The next question was about the biggest problem in your work process, but I think you have just described that. What is essential for you personally about your creative process?

The essential for me is that I reach the 'they' that I mentioned before. I want to reach people. My credo is 'I, you, they'. I'm born with something that I feel as a sort of obligation, and that is to touch people. I think that touching people is the most beautiful thing you can possibly do. Because it changes people. And I think that's what an artist should do. The purpose of an artist is not to be rich or successful. He must always be on the sideline, he must caress and hit at the same time.

How do you achieve that?

Firstly, through myself. There is only one way. First the 'I'. Secondly, by making a performance, or a film, or a work of art which is really elaborate and which really communicates something. Is able to touch people. It's very difficult to touch people nowadays. They've seen so much, they are so spoilt. But no matter what, it's a lot of work. To keep searching till the end. I've always believed that the theatre of ritual that I dreamed of would be realized after ten years of work – which is what has happened. I've worked for ten years now, and until now I don't think that I've succeeded in doing what I wanted to do. I've touched some people, but not enough. So I think I'm going to have to keep doing this until the end.

Dreams

What would you change or try out in a rehearsal process, if anything was possible?

I think that I still have a lot to learn. I master what I do, but I can see that there are so many other ways of doing it, and I don't know them yet. It's always interesting to see how something can be done better. It's an apprenticeship that I do while working, so to speak. But I can't name a particular strategy, a form of theatre or a form of rehearsal that I haven't tried and that I think might be the solution for my work.

I tried it two years ago – this project that was very difficult. I wanted to do something that I had never done before, work with the actors without preparation, without anything, go ahead, try. Have fun. It didn't work. So I went back to my own way of working. I think that what I do is so personal and unique in its genre that I need to do it my way and do it organically. Organically and very organized at the same time. I write, I make plans, I draw. And based on that we work. Sometimes I've watched other people's rehearsals and I see how they work, and I know that I could never do it like that. Still, I'm very curious about how others do. I just find it very difficult to use it for myself. I often include a new element in my projects, for example putting an orchestra on stage. I had never worked with an orchestra before, but I do that especially to learn how to work with them. To see how it's done technically, to meet new people that will explain to me how it works – that has worked well every time. And it's done because the project requires it. I don't want to do anything that's not required. If the project doesn't require that I work with another method, then I won't. I try to include new elements because they will make it necessary for me to work in new ways. But 80 per cent of the time I work the same way that I have always done, and 20 per cent is new, working with new elements. I also work differently with different people. With each person it's a different kind of professional relation.

So, saying that there is a utopian dream in my life – no. My only regret is that in my education in general there hasn't been enough focus on producing something or learning a craft. That there weren't any schools for directors from the age of twelve. You learn too late what it is. In sports, we find it completely normal to begin when you are eight in order to become someone… I think you need ten years to become a master of what you do, and ten years of working intensively, not just a little bit, but every day. You can become a master of anything you want, I think. Even without talent. And those with talent become the greatest inspirators. It is really a shame that this is not part of children's education. It's always math, and history, and all that, which is fine, but I would have liked to have learned something that had to do with art.

I wish I could have known [Jacques] Brel or just seen him in real life and talked to him. I even dreamt once that Brel was sitting next to me in my car and explained something to me, strange, but… He is a real inspiration for me. I sometimes regret, when I see artists, directors that I think are brilliant, that I don't have the chance to meet them. It's so difficult, they are far away and you have to be famous yourself to get to meet them. I just really wish that I could talk to these people. Lars von Trier is incredible, I think. A genius. The best director there is at the moment. Oh, and he's Danish, too! Björk I find incredible… I would have like to have met [Stanley] Kubrick, he was amazing. Frankly, it's the film directors that interest me. Not so much the theatre directors. Especially not the avant-garde theatre, it really doesn't touch me. I don't really feel like a theatre director [*laughs*]. I use theatre a little bit, but I'm not really a theatre director.

Interview: Isabelle Reynaud

Wayn Traub (BE)
Wayn Traub (born 1972) is a director, filmmaker, choreographer and performer. In the late nineties he published his *Manifesto for an Animal and Ritual Theatre*, and his creative work is characterized by the desire to explore a modern ritual theatre. He uses text, music, narrative, set and film to produce a polyphonic whole. In 2012, Traub stopped making theatre performances and turned his focus to multimedia works.

Select works
Beasts (1999)
Jean-Baptiste (2004)
Maria-Magdalena (2009)
Petrus the Roman (2012)

Notes on contributors

Co-creators of the project Rehearsal Matters

Barbara Simonsen (DK) is director, dramaturg and artistic director and founder of Seachange Lab (formerly Laboratoriet) in Aarhus, Denmark, an independent and international centre for practical artistic research and performing arts experiments. Born in 1967, she holds a Masters in Comparative Literature and Dramaturgy from Aarhus University and has taught in the Aarhus University departments of Dramaturgy, Comparative Literature and Aesthetics and Culture. In 2004, Simonsen founded Det Andet Teater (The Other Theatre), known as Teater Seachange since 2016, where her experimental productions range from audioplays in cinemas to international music theatre and interactive installations. Simonsen has worked for many years as consultant and facilitator for directors, playwrights, choreographers and companies, specializing in the analysis and development of process, tools and methods.

Website: www.teaterseachange.dk

Isabelle Reynaud (DE/DK) is a director, teacher, and founder and artistic director of Carbon – Theatre, Film and Installation. Born in 1964 in Heidelberg, she grew up in both Germany and France and has lived in Denmark since 1990. Her work as an independent director since 1992 has moved from magic realism to documentary theatre, installations and films with themes like alcoholism, rape, narcissism and women's rights. Her projects stem from a personal and/or political necessity. In addition to her artistic work, Reynaud teaches within the subjects of acting, directing, performing arts methods and cultural understanding. At Laboratoriet/Seachange Lab, Reynaud has been part of the artistic management and worked as a project manager, researcher and facilitator in numerous experiments from 2005 to 2014.

Website: www.isabellereynaud.com

Deborah Vlaeymans (BE/DK) is an electronic music composer, performance artist and dramaturg. Born 1975 in Antwerp, Belgium, she has lived in Denmark since 1998 and holds a Masters in Philosophy and Dramaturgy from Aarhus University and Gent University. Vlaeymans develops audio-visual installations and music compositions for the stage, mainly by tweaking software and sampling through her own field recordings. As a performance artist she has created numerous experimental 'club performances' using elements from pop-culture in a perplexing visual language. Since 2012, Vlaeymans collaborates on performances and installations that combine soundscapes with new technology and software art. At Laboratoriet/Seachange Lab, Vlaeymans worked as coordinator, production manager, researcher and facilitator from 2006 to 2011.

Website: www.deborah.vlaeymans.name

Appendix of interview dates and translators

Chapter 1 Annabel Arden: London, May 2010

Chapter 2 Eugenio Barba: Holstebro, October 2008
Translation: Barbara Simonsen

Chapter 3 Jérôme Bel: Aarhus, September 2009
Translation: Barbara Simonsen

Chapter 4 Rachel Chavkin: New York, March 2016

Chapter 5 Kirsten Dehlholm: Copenhagen, May 2009
Translation: Barbara Simonsen

Chapter 6 Maxine Doyle: London, May 2010

Chapter 7 Jan Fabre: Antwerp, January 2009
Translation: Deborah Vlaeymans and Barbara Simonsen

Chapter 8 Richard Foreman: New York, April 2009

Chapter 9 Heiner Goebbels: Giessen, June 2008
Translation: Barbara Simonsen. The text has been revised by Heiner Goebbels after the original, filmed interview

Chapter 10 Helgard Haug: Berlin, March 2010
Translation: Barbara Simonsen

Chapter 11 Bojan Jablanovec: Aarhus, June 2010

Chapter 12 Elizabeth LeCompte: New York, March 2016

Chapter 13 Richard Lowdon: Aarhus, June 2008

Chapter 14 Soheil Parsa: Toronto, January 2009

Chapter 15 Diane Paulus: New York, March 2016

Chapter 16 Catherine Poher: Copenhagen, February 2010
Translation: Barbara Simonsen

Chapter 17 Berit Stumpf and Sean Patten: Aarhus, August 2008
Translation of German passages: Barbara Simonsen

Chapter 18 Wayn Traub: Antwerp, January 2009
Translation: Barbara Simonsen

Index